PENNINE MOTOR SERVICES
1925-2000

DONALD BINNS

The first vehicles purchased by Pennine were three Overland 14 seat buses followed in 1926 by a single Leyland Leveret seating 20. Two larger normal control Leyland Lionesses - WW 154 and WW 1174 followed in 1927 and these had an increased seating capacity of 26 passengers each. The second of these was photographed outside Skipton Castle when new and carried the first Pennine livery which was maroon with gold lining and scroll ownership. Pennine collection

Designed and Published by Donald Binns(Trackside Publications), 50 Long Meadow, Skipton, North Yorkshire, England, BD23 1BW.
Printed by Amadeus Press Ltd, 517 Leeds Road, Huddersfield, West Yorkshire, HD2 1YJ

Telephone: GARGRAVE 15.

Telegrams: "PENNINE, GARGRAVE."

Garages: WEST STREET, GARGRAVE.
ALBION SQUARE, SKIPTON.
NEW ROAD, INGLETON.

Pennine Motor Services

SALOON MOTOR COACH and OMNIBUS PROPRIETORS.

MOTOR EXCURSIONS and TOURS a SPECIALITY.

Head Office and Works:

YOUR REF.

HIGH STREET,

OUR REF.

GARGRAVE, ...193
VIA LEEDS.

We are indebted to Donald Binns of Trackside Publications for his efforts in producing such a comprehensive history of Pennine Motor Services whose 75th anniversary will be celebrated on Christmas Eve in the year 2000.

Unfortunately it would be impossible to mention all of those who over the years have worked and contributed to the success of this small rural bus company. For our part we have never forgotten that our survival in the beginning was due to the loyalty and support of the local people in the villages we served.

Until last year we alone subsidised our bus services in Craven and perhaps at last times are changing and the public will get an improved rural service from the politicians who from December 1998 have offered some assistance.

Norman Simpson(Partner)
Gargrave 1/10/99

Mr Norman Simpson, Partner in Pennine Motor Services, was photographed standing beside one of his 44 seat Leyland National buses in October 1999. H.Meyer

INTRODUCTION

My interest in Pennine buses goes way back to 1943 when I first started attending Ermysteds Grammar School on Gargrave Road in Skipton. Most of the orange, black and grey liveried vehicles then in use looked positively old-fashioned and indeed they were, mostly dating back to 1929-30. Over the years I have watched the progress of Pennine through good and not so good times. After the War because of a shortage of new vehicles, some buses were re-bodied, others were purchased second-hand and eventually all these earlier remaining buses were replaced. During the 1950s and 1960s Pennine became an operator of top class new vehicles. During the 1970s times changed resulting in a fleet of Leyland/Plaxton bodied coach types used as dual purpose vehicles, some new, some second-hand. More recent unhappy experiences with two new Leyland Swift buses decided Pennine on its present course of purchasing used Leyland National vehicles until today the Company has 16 plus two older remaining Leyland/Plaxton's.

When I first met Mr Norman Simpson, Partner in Pennine Motor Services, it was obvious that we had similar ideas, Norman wanting to see a reliable and comprehensive record of his Company since its inception. In turn I wanted to produce an accurate historical document with fleet lists, the whole to include over 100 photographs. Through the kindness of Norman Simpson, this book has been able to go into considerable detail particularly with regard to the early years and for access to Pennine records I am indebted to Norman who has been enthusiastic about the whole project. With regard to the fleet lists published in this book, we feel these are as accurate as they can be but it must be stated that our lists correct some entries from those previously published. From the records which survive, there remain a few queries to which it has not been possible to produce definite answers and where this occurs we have said so.

Further thanks are due to Norman Simpson for allowing us to use photographs from the Pennine collection and we have noted these in the credits. Few of the pictures in the Pennine collection carry credits and we have used some of them without knowing who the original photographer was. Thanks are also due to Pennine Driver Tony Edwards for allowing full use of pictures from his collection. We have had to use a small number of the late R.F.Mack's photographs and have so credited them. Unfortunately we have been unable to trace the where-a-bouts of his Pennine collection and trust that the present owners will forgive us for this lapse. Thanks also to F.Holmes, Robin Platt, Peter and Michael Bewes, and Jim Winkley for their contributions. For the modern day photographs I would like to thank Phil Lason and Henry Meyer who went out and took most of his pictures specially for this book. Thanks also to G.Lumb for providing old photographs relating to Ramsden Body Builders and adding to the overall picture.

In conclusion I hope readers and bus enthusiasts alike will enjoy this volume about the men and machines who have since 1925 served the Yorkshire Dales. Long may they continue to do so. Long live Pennine!

Donald Binns — 1 January 2000

PENNINE MOTOR SERVICES
Donald Binns — First Published 2/2000

Outside Front Cover: Passing the Company's offices fronting onto Main Street at Gargrave LN8 - JIL 7417 had been purchased second-hand from Ribble.
H.Meyer

Outside Back Cover Top: JIL 2426 was photographed at Gargrave on a private charter in the late 1990s. This had originally been BTL 485X and was acquired from Wings, Sleaford in 1983. This Leyland/Plaxton still survives at the time of writing(late 1999).
H.Meyer

Outside Back Cover Bottom: Two of the latest arrivals completed and ready for service. Ex-Arriva BYW 367V and 437V. Pennine LN16 and LN15 were photographed at Gargrave at the end of October 1999.
H.Meyer

CONTENTS

Pennine originally issued their tickets from a wood rack as illustrated in the foreground and essential equipment were the clippers which snipped a hole to indicate that the return tickets had been used. Behind, is the latest type of computerised ticket machine, the Almex A90 which is now fitted to the entire fleet. H.Meyer

This was Pennine's first coach which entered service in May 1931. An AEC Regal 1 with a rear entrance coach body by Burlingham, the livery was orange(lower)with a duck-egg blue stripe and an orange and black upper. It was photographed leaving the top of the town at Skipton with Whitakers Cafe and Dobsons chemist behind. The indicator blinds read "Pennine" on one side and "Engaged' on the other. On the left of the High Street looking down is an interesting bus. This appears to be a 20 seat Dennis Ace registered AWT 285 operated by Parkers Malhamdale service. It was new in 1935 in which year Parkers was acquired by Pennine and Ribble. This vehicle was never operated by Pennine so the year of this photograph must have been 1935. In 1937 AWT 285 was sold to Silver Star Motors, Carleton. G.Lumb collection

WW 9817 looking smart in maroon lined in gold was photographed on 10 August 1930 at the Windermere terminus of the Skipton - Windermere Express service. The driver was Bill Chamley.
Pennine collection

The first Pennine bus to run is recorded as a "blue painted Overland, American type with 14 wood seats covered with a type of oil-cloth which easily tore". The service ran between Skipton and Settle five trips each week day and four on Sundays.

Pennine Motor Services was started at 8.30am on Christmas Eve 1925 by the brothers Arthur and Vic Simpson who lived in Ermysted Street, Skipton and brother-in-law Jim Windle. The latter had been a driver for Castle Motors of Skipton working on their Earby and Colne route and he had persuaded the Simpson family to go into the bus business. One of his regular passengers was an insurance agent who frequently discussed the possibility of starting a bus service. Much to his customers disappointment at not being involved, Jim who saw the possibilities of his suggestion, realized that his brothers-in-law had the garage, equipment and expertise to bring such an idea to fruition. The Simpson family were stone masons, builders and paviors in Skipton, building the Methodist Chapel in Gargrave Road and laying the setts in the High Street. This was a skill from which the bus company was to benefit particularly with the planning and construction of such projects as the Red Lion Skipton Garage.

The first Pennine bus was driven by Jim Windle and the starting place in Skipton was outside Dobson's chemist shop just below the Town Hall. Jim Windle knew Mr Dobson and felt at ease using the setts outside his shop. No tickets were issued on that first run and the actual timetable had been devised with a Miss McKell in mind. She was a school teacher travelling daily to school between Gargrave and Coniston Cold. There were but three passengers in total and the bus arrived at Settle quite empty. The new service had a modest start with an advertisement placed in the *Craven Herald* newspaper. The name "Pennine" had been dreamed up by Jim Windle with the other partners agreeing, an eminently suitable name for a service running along part of the backbone of England.

Arthur Simpson had trained as an engineer at Dewhurst's mill on Broughton Road in Skipton and whilst there he built his own 1½h.p. engine and carburetor for a motor cycle, the crank case of which was cast locally at Varley's iron foundry. His motor cycle

This late 1920s picture portrays a group of pot-holers stood next to their bus for the day somewhere around Horton-in-Ribblesdale. The bus is a 14-seater and most probably one of the three Overland's which started off the Pennine fleet.
Pennine collection

WW 3322 was a Waveney bodied Star 'Flyer', the only one in the Pennine fleet. This 20 seater was photographed with Hellifield on its destination blind.

Pennine Collection

reached a top speed of 50mph and was belt driven. The registration was U333. At this period Arthur Simpson began to accumulate tools for the future. He was a member of the Territorial Army and was at Redcar when War broke out in 1914. A Colonel England asked if anyone could drive and Arthur claimed that he could. Despite the fact that he had never been in a car he quickly mastered it. At Christmas 1914 his brother Victor Simpson joined up and for a period the two men were together. Arthur was soon taken out of the army because he was a skilled engineer being sent to work at Peter Brotherhood's in Peterborough. After the end of the War Arthur opened a cycle and motorcycle shop operating from premises in the Liberal Buildings, Keighley Road, Skipton.

Victor Simpson had gone through the battles of the Somme and was also at Ypres and finished the War in Germany. De-mob came with a small pension since he had suffered gas poisoning during the War. Victor had been a lines-man mending telephone wires broken by shelling. He was presented with two medals. He had been so impressed by the quality and ability of Army officers who had been to Public School when compared to those who had come up through the ranks that his son Norman was eventually sent to Giggleswick private school. Norman is presently a partner in Pennine Motor Services.

After the War Arthur and Victor joined forces and in 1920 Arthur set his sights on the old laundry in Skipton's Albion Yard. One night he 'helped' the building to collapse and next day he offered to repair it if Captain Fordyce, the Castle Agent, would grant a tenancy. Arthur rebuilt the wall square instead of curved creating a garage and facilities for motorcycles and later for cars. The first car they sold was a Rover to old Dr.Robinson whose sons Lionel and Cedric(also Doctors)were enthusiastic helpers. Albion Garage would also serve the new bus business.

Strange how fate plays its many parts for one day a man with a bowler hat approached Arthur Simpson in Skipton High Street offering him a garage in Gargrave, near the Grouse Hotel. A price was mentioned and following consultation with brother Victor they went to view and lost no time in purchasing it from Norman J.Clarke of Gargrave. From February 1928 the new garage became the Company's head-quarters and re-named Grouse Garage, remains so today. Such was to be their commitment to the bus industry that the Simpson's did not try to run two businesses and even a brand new Ford Model 'T' car was laid to one side and not sold(this was eventually broken up after the Second World War). Jim Windle became the first traffic manager while Arthur and Victor Simpson were responsible for maintaining the buses. As the business grew it was known for the 14-seat bus to pick up over 40 passengers and some had to stand on the running boards, leaning over the bonnet. The 'early' turn started at 6.30am and ended at 10pm. 'Late' turn started at 7.30am and finished at 11pm.

In 1926 the bus industry was new and expansion was possible by means of new routes, excursions into the Dales and to the sea-side resorts, plus private parties - all means of increasing turn-over. Pennine's first bus was a 14-seat charabanc type Overland; two similar additional motor vehicles being added during 1926. Later in 1926 Pennine Motors needed a larger vehicle to supplement the three 14-seater Overland vehicles and the Company visited Leyland Motors Ltd, Lancashire, where they were introduced to a 20-seat normal control all-Leyland *Leveret*, this representing the commencement of a long association with Leyland Motors heralding the first in a long line of 'Animals', *Lions, Tigers* and continuing to the *Leopards* of the 1960s. A 20 seat Star *Flyer*(WW 3322)with a body by Waveney of Lowestoft was also purchased even though the fleet was by then 6 vehicles strong(3 Overland, 3 Leyland). The Star was a 1928 model, delivered late in 1927. It was later sold to Cononley Motors near Skipton. Following that came 5 Leyland *Lions* and 3 *Tigers* before a magnificent AEC *Regal* with coach body was added to the fleet in 1931. Immediately following the Star *Flyer* were 2 long *Lions* with bodies by United Bodybuilders(WW5185/6). These had smoking compartments but for some reason were not liked. A detailed fleet list for the earlier vehicles follows. The fleet lists published in this book have been produced mainly from correspondence and insurance documents in the possesion of Pennine, from photographic records and personal observation. Previously published lists have been ignored. The table which follows details all vehicles acquired between 1925 and 1939 and includes vehicles confirmed as definite and also the few which are on the Pennine list but for which there is doubt.

Please refer to the notes at the end of the table for further clarification.

ACQUISITIONS 1925-1939

Registration No.	Make	Chassis No.	Body Made By	Type	New	In to Service	Out of Service	Disposal	Notes
WU 3749	Overland	BMT 1957	Warwick	S14F	12/25	12/25	3/30	Scrapped	2
WU 4197	Overland	BMT 2200	Warwick	S14F	1/26	1/26*	9/31	Scrapped	17
WU 6162	Overland	BMT 2682	Warwick	S14F	4/26	4/26*	9/30		
WU 8434	Leyland Leveret	40034	Leyland	S20F	9/26	9/26*	by 2/31	A	3
WW 154	Leyland Lioness	45424	Leyland	S26F	3/27	3/27*	by 11/40	C	16
WW 1174	Leyland Lioness	45466	Leyland	S26F	4/27	4/27*	10/33	C	16
WW 3322	Star Flyer	B775	Waveney	S20F	5/27	5/27*	12/29	D	
WW 5185	Leyland Lion	46614	United	S32F	3/28	3/28*	11/35	C	4
WW 5186	Leyland Lion	46615	United	S32F	3/28	3/28*	3/36	C	4
WW 9531	Leyland Tiger	60338	Leyland	S30F	5/29	5/29*	10/49	Scrapped	1
WW 9817	Leyland Tiger	60339	Leyland	S30F	5/29	5/29*	12/53	Scrapped	1,6
WW 9818	Leyland Tiger	60337	Leyland	S30F	5/29	5/29*	10/40	Scrapped	1
WX 2979	Leyland Lion	50535	Leyland	S30F	2/30	2/30*	4/51	Scrapped	7,15
WX 3735	Leyland Lion	50536	Leyland	S30F	3/30	3/30*	7/51	Scrapped	15
WX 3736	Leyland Lion	50537	Leyland	S30F	4/30	4/30*	12/51		15
WX 7431	AEC Regal 1	662976	Burlingham	C30R	5/31	5/31*	10/57		9
AWX 763	Leyland Tiger	9800	Leyland	S32F	3/36	3/36*	9/54	Scrapped	8,10
AWX 764	Leyland Tiger	9801	Leyland	S32F	3/36	3/36*	10/58	F	8,10,11
WU 9999	Dennis 'E'	17119	Ramsden	S32F	2/27	by 10/30	by 11/40	C	12
YG 3405	Dennis Lancet	170307	Ramsden	S32R	/33	/41	12/53	Scrapped	13
CK 4295	Leyland Tiger	61089	Leyland	S31F	/30	9/38	10/49	Scrapped	5,14
CK 4296	Leyland Tiger	61090	Leyland	S31F	/30	9/38	10/49	Scrapped	5,14
CK 4297	Leyland Tiger	61091	Leyland	S31F	/30	9/38	10/49	Scrapped	5,14

* Purchased New   S = Service Bus   C = Coach   U = Utility Body
R = Rear entrance   F = Front entrance

The following vehicles were on 28 June 1930 registered with Skipton Urban District Council and authorised to operate WU6162, WU 8434, WW 154, WW 1174, WW 5185, WW 5186, WW 9531, WW 9817, WW 9818, WX 2979 and WU 9999.

Notes:

1. Leyland Tiger TS1.
2. Probably bought new.
3. Ex-Leyland demonstrator. PLC 1.
4. Long Lion PLSC. With smoking compartment.
5. Leyland Tiger TS2.
6. Rebodied in the mid 1940s as a coach by H.V.Burlingham, C33F and painted in overall orange.
7. Rebodied with utility body in 1944 by H.V.Burlingham, US32F.
8. Leyland Tiger TS7.
9. Rebodied by H.V.Burlingham as S34F in 1950. Fitted with AEC 7.7 diesel unit 1951.
10. Used by West Riding Ambulance Service during War. Painted grey and fitted as an 8 stretcher ambulance.
11. About 1953 fitted with coach body off WW 9817.
12. Acquired second-hand from A.Hull, Skipton.
13. Acquired second-hand in 1936 from Parkers, Malhamdale service. Rebodied with a 32 seat utility body in 1945 by H.V.Burlingham.
14. Ex-Ribble Motor Services. Acquired second-hand in 1938. With roof-racks and ladders. CK 4304 also purchased for spares.
15. Leyland Lion LT1.
16. Leyland PLC 1.
17. May have been WU 4097.

Disposal:

A. Sold 19/2/31 to Waddington & Evans(there is some doubt as to the actual name), Bolton - by - Bowland M.S.
C. To John H. Hornby & Sons, LNE goods depot Bradford 11/40.
D. To Ratcliffe, Skipton. Sold 23/1/30 and converted to lorry..
F. To Hillcrest, Ingleton.

The following buses also appear on one Pennine list but it has been impossible to confirm their existence: WW 9816 Tiger, WX 2747 Tiger, WX 2980 Lion. These are considered doubtful.

Also:	YG 1285	Dennis Lancet - nothing known. Maybe ex- Parkers Malhamdale service.
	WX 3724	Thornycroft - Ex-Parkers Malhamdale Service. Not put into service with Pennine. Chassis No. 18352. Ramsden body B25F. New 3/30. To John J.Hornby & Sons, Bradford 11/40.
	WU 4540	Ford. Chassis No.1297118. B14. New 3/26. Into service 3/26. Out of service /30. Scrapped 3/31. Ex-Arthur Hull.According to Norman Simpson Pennine never bought or ran a Ford on service. Other 14 seaters owned by Hull were not taken into Pennine stock.
	AWT 285	Dennis Ace. Chassis No.200141. Type S20F. Acquired with the purchase of Parkers Malhamdale service. Never run by Pennine and sold to J.T. Hey, Silver Star, Carleton in 1937 and thence to West Yorkshire Road Car Co., in 1943 for spares.

WW
5185
Pennine

CHEMIST
INGLETON
WW 9531

Opposite Page Top: If only photographs could talk! Unfortunately little is known about the event - possibly just a gathering for a snap-shot. On the left is WW 5185 one of the pair of 1928 Long Lions with United bodies incorporating a smoking compartment. Of the bus body on its side nothing is known, nor of the chassis on the right. Seated(right)is A.V.Simpson with behind him E.Collings, then left in drivers uniform Harry Addyman, and to his left Percy Shuttleworth. Next to him on his left at the back, Harry Fletcher and in front Edgar Smith, then Joe Hargreaves and A.D.Simpson seated.

Pennine collection

Opposite Page Bottom: A 1929 Leyland Tiger WW 9531 rests outside the first Skipton departure point on the Setts outside Dobsons Chemist shop just below the Town Hall. The destination indicator shows 'Ingleton'. The livery is maroon with gold leaf lettering.

Tony Edwards collection

(ACCIDENT)

No. L.3237.

COVER NOTE.

Port of Manchester Insurance Co. Limited.

Head Office: 4, ALBERT SQUARE, MANCHESTER.

Class.

Motor Vehicle.

Particulars.

Comprenehsive Cover, on vehtcles described on reverse side, plus unlimited passenger indemnity.

Messrs. Simpson Bros, T/A Pennine Motor Services, and Ebor Trading Co. for their resp. rights and interests being desirous to effect an Insurance in accordance with particulars shewn hereon, and having this Third day of April 1930 deposited £ ----- on account of the Premium, is/are hereby held insured (subject to the terms and conditions of the Company's Policy applicable to such form of Insurance) until the Policy is issued, or notice given that the Insurance is declined, but in any case for not more than fourteen days from the date hereof.

The Company will charge a proportion of the Annual Premium in respect of the period during which it has been on risk.

Branch Manager.

ATTACHING TO AND FORMING PART OF POLICY NO - M.V.B.16231.

Make.	Seats.	H.P.	Year.	Cost.	Bought.	Value.	Registered.
Leyland Leveret.	20.	22.	1926.	£1080.	1926.	£700.	W.U.843[illegible]
Leyland Lioness.	26.	29.	1927.	£1375.	1927.	£900.	W.W. 154.
Leyland Lioness.	26.	29.	1927.	£1375.	1927.	£900.	W.W.1174.
Dennis.	32.	40.	1927.	£1200.	1927.	£850.	W.U.9999.
Leyland Lion.	32.	30.	1928.	£1455.	1928.	£950.	W.W.5185.
Leyland Lion.	32.	30.	1928.	£1455.	1928.	£950.	W.W.5186.
Leyland Tiger.	30.	40.	1929.	£1800.	1929.	£1600.	W.W.9531.
Leyland Tiger.	30.	40.	1929.	£1800.	1929.	£1600.	W.W.9817.
Leyland Tiger.	30.	40.	1929.	£1800.	1929.	£1600.	W.W.9818.
Leyland Lion.	30.	30.	1930.	£1552.	1930.	£1500.	W.X.2979.
Leyland Lion.	30.	30.	1930.	£1545.	1930.	£1545.	W.X.3735.
Leyland Lion.	30	30.	1930.	£1545.	1930.	£1545.	W.X.3736.

All used for Public and Private Hire.

Memo- It is hereby declared and agreed that this policy extends to indemnify the County Council of the West Riding of Yorkshire under Section 1 (Liability to the Public), whilst the within mentioned vehicle is being used under Contract with the said County Council for the conveyance of Schoolchildren, and further this this Policy extends to indemnify the said County Council in the event of any claim being made against them by Schoolchildren being so conveyed.

Entered in the office books this 14th day of May 1930.

For JOSEPH PERDUE.
GENERAL MANAGER.

Buses of that time were of course petrol-engined and a regular supply of that fuel was sourced. The best price was obtained on Russian Oil Products, the petrol being delivered in barrels. The Overland, a light vehicle ran happily on a tank full - 6 gallons per day. When a petrol pump was installed in Skipton, it was manually operated delivering half-a-gallon at a time - fuelling the bus was a slow process.

SUMMARY OF MILES RUN, EARNINGS, PETROL AND OIL USED JANUARY 1927

BUS OVERLAND No. 1

Week	Miles Run	Earnings £ - s - d	Petrol used gallons.	Oil used pints.
1	943	17-0-0	47	16
2	1079	19-13-9	51	17
3	1008	18-7-9	52	18
4	374*	8-4-2	17	6
5	96▲	1-13-1	-	-

* Not running 3 days. 4 day week only.
▲ Not running 1 day. 2 day week only.

OVERLAND No. 2

Week	Miles Run	Earnings £ - s - d	Petrol used gallons.	Oil used pints.
1	1064	24-0-6	53	13
2	1047	20-10-9	46½	14
3	1066	21-2-9	54½	13
4	988	18-12-5½	38½	9
5	404†	10-5-1½	16	4

† 3 day week. end of month.

BUS OVERLAND No.3

Week	Miles Run.	Earnings £ - s - d	Petrol used gallons.	Oil used pints.
1	298*	4-11-0	13½	4
2	*			
3	*			
4	808	11-17-5	45½	20
5	276†	10-7-7	?	?

* Worked 2 days. On third day ran from Skipton to Trafford Park to body-builders for painting(Warwick Manchester). 43 miles, 7 gallons, 2 pints.
On 21st returned from Trafford Park to Skipton. Ran one trip to Hellifield. 63 miles, 2 gallons.

† 3 day week - end of month.

MARCH 1927

BUS LEYLAND LIONESS No. 5

Week	Miles Run.	Earnings £ -s - d	Petrol used gallons.	Oil used pints.
1	594	27-12-5	80	2
2	512	21-9-11	67	2
3	648	23-19-0	82	2
4	512	21-9-4	52	-

Bus worked 6 days per week, 1 day off.

TOTAL RECEIPTS FROM TICKET SALES AND MILEAGE OF ALL BUSES - JANUARY 1927

Date of month.	Daily Mileage	Daily Total Receipts	Weekly Total Mileage	Weekly Total Receipts
1	640	18-12-9		
2	372	6-13-9		
3	395	11-7-3		
4	433	10-1-0		
5	402	8-12-6		
6	448	7-14-10		
7	404	6-11-0	3094	£69-13-1
8	592	17-6-6		
9	308	6-10-6		
10	392	7-12-3		
11	443	9-18-9		
12	402	8-19-0		
13	412	10-4-0		
14	427	8-5-0	2976	£68-16-0
15	544	16-16-3		
16	320	6-18-6		
17	340	7-9-9		
18	554	16-11-6		
19	372	9-4-9		
20	392	7-5-0		
21	392	4-18-3	2914	£69-4-0
22	640	16-15-6		
23	340	7-7-3		
24	381	10-0-4		
25	366	10-5-9½		
26	392	6-3-1½		
27	441	7-3-0½		
28	426	6-4-3	2986	£69-19-3½
29	600	18-2-11		
30	340	6-17-5½		
31	372	10-11-3½		

continued into February.

At this period there were three Overland's and one Leveret.

The bus in the early years gave people a new mobility and a wider choice of employment. People were able to travel daily into town for work in shops, cafes, offices and industry. Men could leave the land to work in the mills and factories and in the evening the new entertainment - the picture house - was there upon which to spend the new wealth. It was not uncommon for 75 people to get off a 26 seater bus. On one occasion the driver Henry Fletcher when asked by the local police Sergeant where they were all coming from replied "they were running behind the bus having got out of the emergency door at the back".

Before the establishment of Pennine Motor Services there was already a regular bus service between Skipton and Gargrave operated by Mr Arthur Hull(of Skipton)who ran his first bus in 1921. Arthur Hull was a pioneer in the bus world. His first bus a 14 seater Ford was provided with a step ladder, placed at the rear and

This vehicle was WU 9999, a Dennis 'E' type new in 1927 to Arthur Hull, Gargrave, It had a 32 seat front entrance bus body by Joseph Ramsden Ltd, of Liversedge, near Bradford and was built for one-man operation. Hull's business was purchased by Pennine in 1927 but some three years later this bus was out of service. It was not scrapped but in 1940 was sold to a Bradford concern. This photograph is especially interesting in that it poses a problem. Firstly this is obviously a works photograph taken when the bus was new, but note that it carries boards beneath the windows proclaiming a Skipton - Settle service. Mr Norman Simpson(of Pennine)stated that Pennine were the only operator and Arthur Hull never ran to Settle from Skipton. It looks though as if Arthur Hull had other ideas! G.Lumb collection

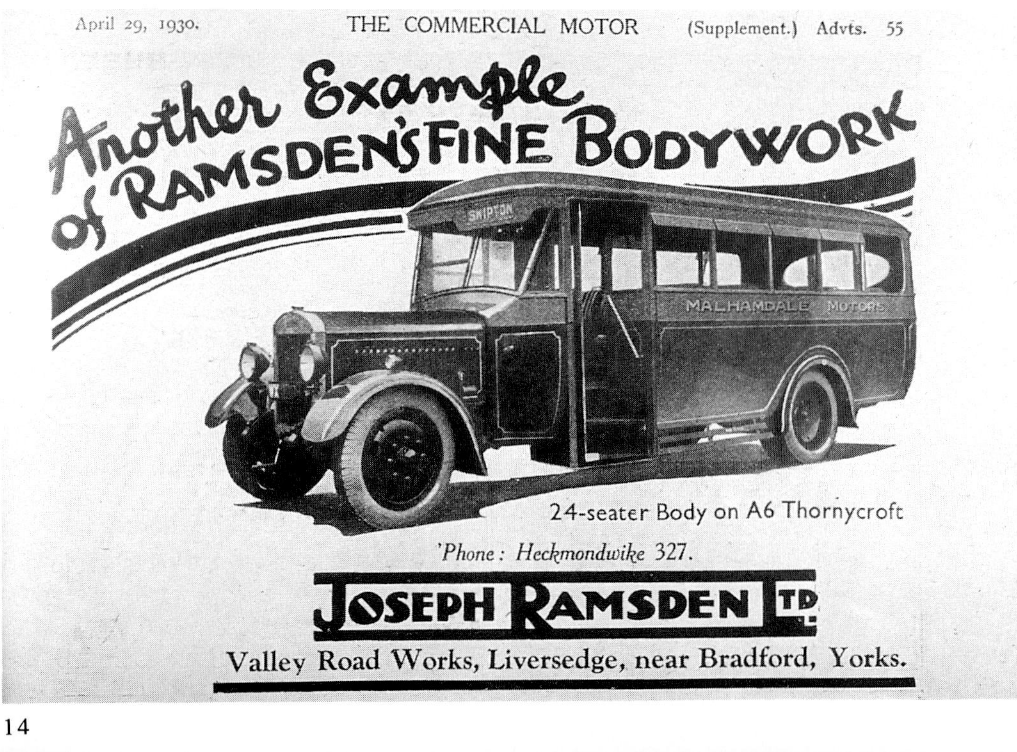

Joseph Ramsden Ltd., placed this advert in "The Commercial Motor" supplement for 29 April 1930. The bus illustrated is a Thornycroft of Malhamdale Motors - see page 22. G.Lumb collection

Another 1929 Leyland Tiger WW 9817 was photographed at the Windermere terminus of the Skipton - Windermere express service on 10 August 1930. The service was short-lived and finished on 21 September 1930. The driver was Bill Chamley. The livery is still maroon with gold leaf lettering. The Windermere run was a regular Sunday morning summer service and when WW 9531(shown in photograph on Page 10)was brought home to Gargrave by A.D.Simpson when new, it carried 'Windermere' on the destination screen. Pennine collection

removed to the side of the bus when passengers got in, and out. On the side were the words "It'll be reet". His third bus - a 20 seater, was soon in trouble with the cone clutch, and Hull had to dig a hole in the ground to get at it. It was not long after receiving this bus that he decided to sell out. Pennine paid £2000 and the new bus, which was on the never - was taken over. Hull demanded payment in cash and this was arranged with Martins Bank. The Dennis was hardly used because its Cone clutch was very heavy to withdraw and required both feet to depress. It was not popular and so was laid up at the bottom of the garage for a long period with the gearbox out. It never ran again.

Hull had his bus stand infront of the Old George Hotel in Skipton and his wife took her turn at driving. An amazing, but true tale was told by Tom Wade, Arthur Hulls' first driver. He was driving in a heavy fog from Gargrave to Skipton and there were several fishermen on the bus and Tom could not see where he was going. One fisherman had the bright idea of putting his fishing rod outside to tell him how far he was from the side of the road, and he commanded the driver by saying "in a bit", "out a bit". However going down Gargrave Road he caught a man under the chin, so that was the end of the bright idea, the man was laid out on the footpath.

Tom Wade joined Pennine when Hulls service was acquired. Tom had to pass his driving test, the PSV Examiner was about to take him on the road when Tom's masterful way of starting up got him passed straight away, no self-starter in those days. Many a driver got a wollop when the engine kicked back. Pennine records indicate that Hull's new bus was an 'E' type Dennis and its registration number was WU9999 and not as generally thought WW9999. It was not as recorded in various magazine articles a *Lance 1* but a 32 seat 'E' type. The forward control body was originally for one-man operation and built by Ramsdens of Liversedge who also built the body of the later ex-Malhamdale Dennis *Lance 1* YG 3405. It is believed that the original livery of WU9999 was chocolate and cream. The 1927 purchase of Mr Hull's business and new Dennis 'E', gave Pennine sole occupancy of the Gargrave - Skipton route.

An earlier purchase made in 1926 was that of Richard and John Lamb of Settle whose services ran from Settle to Ingleton and Settle to Horton-in-Ribblesdale. They had bad luck with a new 20 seat Minerva bus with moquette seats - for some reason it caught fire and burned completely out on Clapham Common - a great loss, it was a fine machine according to existing records. This acquisition allowed Pennine to extend beyond Settle to Ingleton and after Ribble came to Skipton, to Morecambe. No vehicles were involved in this transaction.

About the same time Ribble Motors, of Preston, extended into the Skipton area from East Lancashire by purchasing Castle Motors, of Skipton(they had started a service into Lancashire in 1924)and this was competition which Pennine Motors could not buy out. From starting with one vehicle in 1925 the Company had purchased 16 new vehicles in the period 1925-1931, plus one additional vehicle aquired with the Hull takeover. On the matter of un-necessary competition with Ribble, Pennine had this to say:

"Competition was very severe in the early days. About 1928 County Motors', Lancaster, started operating three trips daily between Lancaster and Skipton and they tried hard with reduced fares, and running at the same time as Pennine, to get control of the route. County buses were blue and white. Arthur Hull ran 14 seaters(Fords)from Gargrave to Skipton. Pennine charged 5d.each way from Gargrave to Skipton with no returns. Lambs of Settle ran Settle - Ingleton. Parker Bros. ran Malham - Skipton 4 days a week, Easter, Whitsuntide and special occasions or whenever he felt like it. So there was plenty of competition. Even though competition was severe in the late 1920s when County Motors commenced running through to Skipton, there was considerable co-operation between County and Pennine. The following extracts show tickets booked by Pennine to County destinations(table A)and tickets sold by County to Pennine destinations(table B)with the amounts owing to each company.

TICKETS BOOKED BY PENNINE TO COUNTY DESTINATIONS

Period unknown probably one week:

Table A:

Ticket No.	From	To		We owe County	Value
4378	Skipton	Morecambe	Return	3/9d	8/2d
4379	Skipton	Morecambe	Return	3/9d	8/2d
4380	Skipton	Morecambe	Return	3/9d	8/2d
4381	Skipton	Morecambe	Return	3/9d	8/2d
4382	Austwick	Lancaster	Return	3/-d	4/2d
4383	Austwick	Morecambe	Return	3/9d	4/11d
4384	Skipton	Lancaster	Return	3/-d	7/5d
4385	Skipton	Lancaster	Return	3/-d	7/5d
4386	Skipton	Kirby	Return	1/7d	6/-d
4387	Clapham	Lancaster	Return	3/-d	3/9d
4388	Clapham	Lancaster	Return	3/-d	3/9d
4389	Clapham	Bentham	Single	5d	11d
4390	Clapham	Bentham	Single	5d	11d
4391	Settle	Bentham	Single	5d	1/7d
4392	Clapham	Bentham	Single	5d	11d
4393	Clapham	Bentham	Single	5d	11d
4394	Clapham	Bentham	Single	5d	11d
4395	Clapham	Bentham	Single	5d	11d
4396	Skipton	Lancaster	Return	3/-d	7/5d
4397	Skipton	Lancaster	Return	3/-d	7/5d
4398	Gargrave	Lancaster	Return	3/-d	6/9d
				£2-7-3d	

TICKETS BOOKED BY COUNTY MOTORS TO PENNINE DESTINATIONS

Period unknown probably one week:

TABLE B:

Ticket No.	From	To		County owe us	Value
603	Lancaster	Austwick	Return	1/2d	4/2d
604	Lancaster	Skipton	Return	4/6d	7/5d
605	High Bentham	Austwick	Single	9d	1/2d
607	Lancaster	Skipton	Return	4/6d	7/5d
608	Brook House	Long Preston	Return	2/5d	4/8d
609	High Bentham	Clapham	Return	10d	1/7d
610	Lancaster	Skipton	Return	4/6d	7/5d
613	Lancaster	Clapham	Return	9d	3/9d
614	Lancaster	Clapham	Return	9d	3/9d
615	Fourlands	Austwick	Single	9d	1/-d
618	Lancaster	Skipton	Return	4/6d	7/5d
619	Lancaster	Skipton	Return	4/6d	7/5d
2134	Lancaster	Long Preston	Single	1/7d	3/7d
621	Lancaster	Skipton	Single	2/11d	4/11d
602	Lancaster	Austwick	Return	1/2d	4/2d
617	Lancaster	Austwick	Return	1/2d	4/2d
2021	Lancaster	Skipton	Return	4/6d	7/5d
2023	Lancaster	Skipton	Single	2/11d	4/11d
2024	Bentham	Skipton	Single	2/11d	3/2d
2025	Lancaster	Skipton	Return	4/6d	7/5d
2026	Lancaster	Skipton	Return	4/6d	7/5d
				£2-15-5	

We apologise for the poor quality of this photograph but it is interesting in that it probably is one of the two first Leyland Lion's purchased new in 1928. These had United bodies with a smoking compartment.

Tony Edwards collection

SINGLE FARES.

Malham									
3d.	Kirkby Malham								
5d.	3d.	Airton							
7d.	5d.	2d.	Newfield Guest House						
9d.	7d.	4d.	2d.	Eshton Top					
10d	8d.	5d.	3d.	1d.	Eshton				
11d.	9d.	6d.	5d.	3d.	2d.	Gargrave			
1/2	1/-	10d.	8d.	6d.	5d.	3d.	Thorlby		
1/3	1/1	11d.	9d.	7d.	6d.	4d.	1d.	Stirton	
1/4	1/2	1/-	10d.	8d.	7d.	5d.	3d.	2d.	Skipton

RETURN FARES.

Malham									
5d.	Kirkby Malham								
7d.	5d.	Airton							
9d.	...	...	Newfield Guest House						
...	...	...	...	Eshton Top					
...	...	...	...	...	Eshton				
1/5	1/2	11d.	...	...	...	Gargrave			
...	...	...	...	...	...	...	Thorlby		
...	...	...	...	...	...	...	...	Stirton	
2/-	1/10	1/8	1/6	1/2	1/-	8d.	5d.	3d.	Skipton

Malhamdale 'Bus Services

Proprietors:

PARKER BROS., AIRTON,

Near Skipton.

Tel. Airton 3.

Summer Service

Commencing

MAY 30TH, 1936,

Until further notice.

The Craven Herald Limited, Skipton.

MALHAM TO SKIPTON.

MONDAY to FRIDAY.	a.m.	a.m.	p.m.	p.m.	p.m.	p.m.	p.m.	p.m.
Malham .... dep.	7 45	9 35	12 5	1 45	3 15	5 0	6 45	8B20
Kirkby Malham	7 50	9 40	1210	1 50	3 20	5 8	6 50	8B25
Airton	8 0	9 50	1220	2 0	3 30	5 10	7 0	8B30
Newfield (Guest House)	8 2	9 52	1222	2 2	3 32	5 12	7 2	8B32
Eshton Top	8 5	9 55	1225	2 5	3 35	5 15	7 5	8B35
Eshton	8 10	10 0	1230	2 10	3 40	5 20	7 10	8B40
Gargrave (Bond End)	8 15	10 5	1235	2 15	3 45	5 25	7 15	8B45
Skipton (High St.) .... arr.	8 28	1018	1248	2 28	3 58	5 38	7 28	8B58

Reference
B—Wednesday Only.

SATURDAY.	a.m.	a.m.	a.m.	p.m.	p.m.	p.m.	p.m.	p.m.	p.m.	p.m.
Malham .... dep.	7 45	9 45	1130	1 0	2 30	4 0	5 30	7 0	8 30	10 0
Kirkby Malham	7 50	9 50	1135	1 5	2 35	4 5	5 35	7 5	8 35	10 5
Airton	8 0	10 0	1145	1 15	2 45	4 15	5 45	7 15	8 45	1015
Newfield (Guest House)	8 2	10 2	1147	1 17	2 47	4 17	5 47	7 17	8 47	1017
Eshton Top	8 5	10 5	1150	1 20	2 50	4 20	5 50	7 20	8 50	1020
Eshton	8 10	1010	1155	1 25	2 55	4 25	5 55	7 25	8 55	1025
Gargrave (Bond End)	8 15	1015	12 0	1 30	3 0	4 30	6 0	7 30	9 0	1030
Skipton (High St.) .... arr.	8 28	1028	1213	1 43	3 13	4 43	6 13	7 43	9 13	1043

SUNDAY.	a.m.	p.m.	p.m.	p.m.						
Malham .... dep.	...	...	6 15	8 0	...	...	...	...	...	...
Kirkby Malham	...	...	6 20	8 5	...	...	...	...	...	...
Airton	9 45	1 30	6 30	8 15	...	...	...	...	...	...
Newfield (Guest House)	9 47	1 32	6 32	8 17	...	...	...	...	...	...
Eshton Top	9 50	1 35	6 35	8 20	...	...	...	...	...	...
Eshton	9 55	1 40	6 40	8 25	...	...	...	...	...	...
Gargrave (Bond End)	10 0	1 45	6 45	8 30	...	...	...	...	...	...
Skipton (High St.) .... arr.	1013	1 58	6 58	8 43	...	...	...	...	...	...

SKIPTON MALHAM.

MONDAY to FRIDAY.	a.m.	a.m.	p.m.	p.m.	p.m.	p.m.	p.m.	p.m.		
SKIPTON (High St.)......dep.	8 45	1115	1 0	2 32	4 10	5 40	7 35	9E45		
Gargrave (Bond End).........	8 58	1128	1 15	2 46	4 23	5 58	7 48	9E58		
Eshton	9 5	1135	1 20	2 52	4 30	6 0	7 55	10E 5		
Eshton Top	9 10	1140	1 23	2 57	4 35	6 5	8 0	10E10		
Newfield (Guest House)	9 13	1143	1 25	3 0	4 38	6 8	8 3	10E13		
Airton	9 15	1145	1 30	3 2	4 40	6 10	8 5	10E15		
Kirkby Malham	9 20	1150	1 35	3 7	4 45	6 15	8 10	10E20		
Malham ....arr.	9 28	1158	1 40	3 14	4 53	6 23	8 18	10E28		
SATURDAY.	a.m.	a.m.	p.m.	p.m.	p.m.	p.m.	p.m.	p.m.	p.m.	p.m.
Skipton (High St.).........dep.	8 45	1045	1215	1 47	3 15	4 45	6 17	7 47	9 15	1055
Gargrave (Bond End).........	8 58	1058	1228	2 0	3 28	4 58	6 30	8 0	9 28	11 8
Eshton	9 5	11 5	1235	2 7	3 35	5 5	6 37	8 7	9 35	1115
Eshton Top	9 10	1110	1240	2 12	3 40	5 10	6 42	8 12	9 40	1120
Newfield (Guest House)	9 13	1113	1243	2 15	3 43	5 13	6 45	8 15	9 43	1123
Airton	9 15	1115	1245	2 17	3 45	5 15	6 47	8 17	9 45	1125
Kirkby Malham	9 20	1120	1250	2 22	3 50	5 20	6 52	8 22	9 50	1130
Malham ....arr.	9 28	1128	1258	2 30	3 58	5 28	7 0	8 30	9 58	1138
SUNDAY.	a.m.	p.m.	p.m.	p.m.						
Skipton (High St.).........dep.	1030	2 15	7 0	8 45	...	...	...	...	...	...
Gargrave (Bond End).........	1043	2 28	7 13	8 58	...	...	...	...	...	...
Eshton	1050	2 35	7 20	9 5	...	...	...	...	...	...
Eshton Top	1055	2 40	7 25	9 10	...	...	...	...	...	...
Newfield (Guest House)	1058	2 43	7 28	9 13	...	...	...	...	...	...
Airton	11 0	2 45	7 30	9 15	...	...	...	...	...	...
Kirkby Malham	11 5	2 50	7 35	...	...	...	...	...	...	...
Malham ....arr.	1113	2 58	7 43	...	...	...	...	...	...	...

Reference
E—Wednesday Only.

County Motors met with a sad accident on Denny Beck when their bus, being over-loaded, stalled, and ran back into Landholme, killing eight persons and this was the end of County Motors.

It was then that Ribble Motors started to run from Lancaster to Skipton, their fares were for all stages single plus 1d. Pennine Motors never lowered their fares from the beginning because of regular running and courtesy, so much so that the people of Long Preston, Hellifield, Coniston and Gargrave became very loyal.

Jim Windle, Lionel Thornton and Harry Fletcher(of Pennine)were well liked. It so happened that one Saturday evening at the top of Skipton High Street, the Ribble Assistant General Manager, Mr.Bottomley was with Mr.Yeoman(late of County Motors)when he saw two Pennine buses being followed by a Ribble bus with only two passengers on. He asked how long this had been going on and George Yeoman replied "always". To our surprise on the Monday morning Pennine received a letter from Mr Bottomley asking us if we would grant him an interview at our Gargrave office, re-coordination of bus services. We welcomed the idea and wrote accordingly. In the course of a few days Mr Bottomley came to Gargrave and outlined his proposals which were 50/50 on the joint route, certain provisions regarding seating capacity, one being that no less than 26 seaters had to be run".

Pennine were invited over to their offices where Mr Bottomley, along with Jim Windle, Vic and Arthur agreed to all proposals laid down by him. When we arrived we explained that we had no solicitor with us, and he remarked "you are not doing so bad."

Harold Dryden had been despatched to stay at Lancaster to set up a Lancaster-Morecambe service and to report back. This together with overwhelming public support must have influenced Mr Bottomley to create a joint route as the 1931 Transport Act would seal Pennine in. The outcome was a joint agreement dated January 1931 between Pennine Motors and Ribble with a 50/50 pooling of mileage and monies taken over the route from Skipton to Ingleton and on to Lancaster(in Ribble territory), but under the terms of which Pennine was to remain completely independent. Following the joint agreement Pennine buses could be seen on the route from Skipton to Lancaster almost exclusively east of Ingleton, while Ribble operated westwards, although Pennine did operate five buses daily through to Lancaster and Morecambe. This agreement with Ribble also involved the route from Skipton to Malham from 1936. Also in January 1931 the Traffic Act was ammended and the legal speed limit raised from 12mph to 30mph, a significant improvement.

In November 1932 *Motor Transport* described Pennine's latest licensing application as "an umbrella service, stretching a 'shorts' licence ... This is the most extra-ordinary service I have met yet, said Mr Chamberlain, the Chairman of the North Western Traffic Commissioners at their Manchester sitting. Pennine Motor Services applied for a variation to permit them to terminate their service from Skipton at the LMS Promenade railway station at Morecambe. Mr Chamberlain remarked that the service was a thread on which many other services hung. Applicants applied for a service from Skipton to Morecambe, and ran once a

WW 9818 a 1929 Leyland Tiger, was photographed in maroon livery at Morecambe in June 1930. Pennine collection

day only, but had many intermediate services. Under this umbrella service they sheltered a lot of little ones. It was an outstanding example of what could be done under a 'shorts' licence". They would indicate to the Yorkshire Commissioners what was taking place. The licence was granted but decision was reserved concerning the use of the Promenade station. When Pennine began its Lancaster service in 1930 they parked in Dalton Square but were soon up before the Bench for using County Council office frontage in Lancaster. The Company was fined and the Chairman of the Bench recommended Pennine to use Damside Street which was later developed as the bus station.

In 1933 Pennine started its service to Malham and in 1935 Pennine and Ribble jointly bought the business of Parker Bros., Airton. They had operated from Gargrave, running via Airton up Malhamdale on Wednesday, Saturday and Sundays and at Whitsuntide and Christmas. The service was very unreliable and did not always run. Because of this Mrs Coates from Malham Moor wrote as Secretary of the Womens Institute to request Pennine to operate a regular and reliable service. Two vehicles were taken over by Pennine. One was a 1932 Dennis Lancet with a 32-seat bus body by Ramsdens of Liversedge and this was registered YG 3405. It was retained by Pennine, being re-bodied with a utility style bus body during the 1939-45 War by H.V.Burlingham, of Blackpool. It was also converted to an oil-engine using a Dennis 4-cylinder type. Parker's other bus - a 1935 20-seat Dennis *Ace* was not used but sold locally to Silver Star Motors(J.T.Hey)operating a service from his garage in Carleton, to Skipton. In July 1943 this vehicle - AWT 285 was sold to the West Yorkshire Road Car Company for spares - this fleet operating a handful of these Dennis *Ace* buses with forward projecting bonnets which were always known as 'Flying Pigs'. Parker Bros. livery was maroon and grey.

A number of the early 1930s Leyland vehicles had roof-racks fitted and rear access ladders, but roof-racks were only ever used by the pot-hole club on their outings. According to Pennine records only the three 1930 *Tigers* purchased from Ribble in 1938 were so fitted - none of the early Leylands purchased new had rear ladders and roof-racks. In these early years an hourly service was usually operated between Skipton and Settle with approximately alternate workings through to Ingleton. From there a three hourly service via alternative routes was maintained to Lancaster with one early morning working to and from Morecambe. There were Ribble workings over this section at other times, and on Sundays for several years at least one Ribble vehicle worked throughout from Lancaster to Skipton(twice).

The two photographs on this page are reproduced because they are the only known ones of YG 3405 in original condition. This was a Dennis Lancet with a 32 seat rear-entrance body by Ramsden, of Liversedge. This bus was acquired in 1936 when Pennine purchased Parker's Malhamdale Service and it was to survive the War, being re-bodied in 1945. These pictures were taken as portraits of Pennine employee Jeff Horsman and not for the bus itself. Unfortunately the full front and full side elevations are incomplete. Note the number '210' in the front window indicating this bus was on the Malham service. Photographed just pre-War at Malham.

R.Platt collection

This bus is the one which appears in Joseph Ramsden Ltd., advert reproduced on page 14. It is a Thornycroft of 1930 registered WX 3724 and has a 25 seat Ramsden body. When Parkers Malhamdale service(Malhamdale Motors)was purchased this vehicle was disposed of and did not run for Pennine. Parkers livery was maroon and grey and nicely lined out(in gold?) G.Lumb collection

1929 Leyland Tiger WW 9818 bound for Settle stands next to a Wharfedale Motors bus(probably a Guy)bound for Grassington. On the Setts near Dobson's Chemist on the High Street at Skipton. Tony Edwards collection

MILES RUN IN WEEKS AND TOTAL FARES TAKEN IN £.s.d FOR EACH DRIVER
PERIOD WEEK ENDING 27 MARCH TO WEEK ENDING 8 MAY 1931

		March 27/31		April 3/31		April 10/31	
Driver	No.	Miles	Cash	Miles	Cash	Miles	Cash
Hardiman.W	1	685.8	20-7-3	772.6	26-4-10	696.0	32-9-7
Brown.W	2	666.8	25-0-7	692.3	19-19-1	649.4	29-19-11
Butt.F	3	708.8	19-13-2	812.8	28-0-5	778.4	39-13-7
Staveley.W	4	717.1	21-14-1½	741.1	27-13-2	843.8	48-19-2½
Capstick.E	5	794.8	30-9-2	668.2	24-4-0	794.9	46-12-3
McMinn.W	6	604.4	21-16-1	674.2	23-8-5	623.4	29-5-3
Fletcher.E	7	601.8	20-0-1	648.0	31-11-6½	594.8	33-1-8
Greaves.A	8	750.4	26-6-5	661.6	19-10-11	715.3	49-19-0
Jolly.R	9	216.0	4-12-6	128.8	4-14-11	261.6	16-10-0
Smith.E	10	64.5	4-19-8	54.4	1-5-2	206.2	6-3-8
Addyman.H	11	21.2	1-0-7	23.3	17-9	81.6	2-10-1
		5834.6	£196-2-7½	5777.3	£207-10-2½	6245.4	£335-4-2½

April 17/31		April 24/31		May 1/31		May 8/31	
Miles	Cash	Miles	Cash	Miles	Cash	Miles	Cash
677.1	21-2-4	717.1	22-7-9	664.8	24-3-6	686.7	22-17-8
697-6	22-3-9	678.0	22-2-7	685.6	20-14-0	685.2	26-19-10
664.8	24-17-5	664.8	24-5-7	686.0	24-1-3	844.2	21-5-8
719.2	23-10-11	684.3	22-10-1	794.9	32-8-0	702.3	21-4-2
686.6	23-6-5	794.9	29-14-4½	717.6	22-5-1	794.9	33-2-10
795.0	31-0-10½	706.6	20-17-1	705.8	23-10-7	705.2	25-8-7
656.6	29-9-2	623.4	14-13-8	601.8	28-15-7	626.0	19-0-5
618.8	17-19-7	656.6	25-18-11	637.4	18-7-2	656.6	28-16-9
125.3	5-17-3	81.0	2-8-1	126.0	5-4-2	130.3	3-17-7
-	-	-	-	-	-	8.6	9
-	-	-	-	-	-	-	-
5641.0	£199-7-8½	5506.7	£184-18-1	5588.9	£199-9-4	5840.0	£202-14-3

The following services were operated jointly with Ribble during the pre-second World War years:

Skipton - Gargrave - Hellifield - Settle - Ingleton.
Skipton - Ingleton - Bentham - Wennington - Lancaster and Morecambe. One route ran via Millhouses, a second via the Crazy Cow at Wennington.
Skipton - Gargrave - Airton - Malham.(Parker's route).

The following services were operated by Pennine during the same period:

Skipton - Ingleton - Windermere - Seasonal before 1930(via the 'A6' hence participation in the Leeds - Kendal express service). The Sunday service to Windermere finished on 21 September 1930.
Hellifield - Gisburn - Short period only.

One-man operated. The driver was allowed to take his meal at the Black Horse, Hellifield, however, frequently the takings were insufficient to pay for a drink never mind a meal!

Settle - Rathmel - Tosside - Tuesday only. This route was originally registered as Skipton - Long Preston - Tosside - Wigglesworth - Rathmell - Settle. Then Settle to Rathmell and back to Settle, finally returning from Settle via Rathmell, Wigglesworth, Tosside and Long Preston to Skipton.

Skipton - Gargrave(Johnson & Johnson's works service).

Pennine Motors.

Skipton, Settle, Ingleton, Morecambe.

WEEKDAYS.

(Town Hall)	A.M.	A.M.	A.M.	A.M.	A.M.	P.M.	P.M.	P.M.	P.M.
Skipton ....dep.	6 30	7 45	9 0	1025	1130	1240	1 15	2 25	3* 0
Gargrave	6 45	8 0	9 15	1040	1145	1255	1 30	2 40	3*15
Conistone Cold	6 50	8 5	9 22	1047	1152	1 2	1 37	2 47	3*22
Hellifield..................	7 0	8 15	9 37	11 2	12 7	1 17	1 52	3 2	3*37
Long Preston	7 7	8 23	9 45	1110	1215	1 25	2 0	3 10	3*45
Settle (Market Place) .. arr.	7 20	8 35	10 0	1125	1230	1 40	2 15	3 25	4* 0
Settle (Market Place) ..dep.	7 20	8 35	10 0	..	..	1 40	..	3 25	..
Austwick	7 35	8 50	1015	..	..	1 55	..	3 40	..
Clapham	7 40	9 0	1020	..	..	2 0	..	3 50	..
Newby..................	7 45	9 5	1025	..	..	2 5	..	3 55	..
Ingleton (Inglebr. Htl.) arr.	8 0	9 20	1035	..	..	2 20	..	4 10	..
Ingleton (Inglebro. Htl.) dep.	..	..	1045	..	..	2 30	..	..	..
Burton-in-Lonsdale	..	..	1055	..	..	2 40	..	..	..
Cantsfield	..	..	11 5	..	..	2 50	..	..	..
Melling	..	..	1115	..	..	3 0	..	..	..
Hornby	..	..	1122	..	..	3 7	..	..	..
Claughton	..	..	1130	..	..	3 15	..	..	..
Caton	..	..	1140	..	..	3 25	..	..	..
Lancaster (Dalton Sq.)	..	..	1155	..	..	3 40	..	..	..
Morecambe ....arr.	..	..	1215	..	..	4 0	..	..	..

* Saturdays Only.

SKIPTON TO SETTLE, INGLETON AND MORECAMBE.

WEEKDAYS.—Continued.

(Town Hall)	P.M.	P.M.	P.M.	P.M.	P.M.	P.M.	P.M.	P.M.	P.M.
Skipton ....dep.	3 25	4 30	5 10	6 20	7* 0	8 0	9 5	10 0	11* 5
Gargrave	3 40	4 45	5 25	6 35	7*15	8 15	9 20	10 15	11*20
Conistone Cold	3 47	4 52	5 32	6 42	7*22	8 22	9 27	10 22	11*27
Hellifield..................	4 2	5 7	5 47	6 57	7*37	8 32	9 42	10 37	11*32
Long Preston	4 10	5 15	5 55	7 5	7*45	8 40	9 50	10 45	11*45
Settle ....arr.	4 25	5 30	6 10	7 20	8* 0	9 0	10 5	11 0	12* 0
Settle........ ....dep.	..	..	6 10	..	..	9*15	..	11* 0	..
Austwick	..	..	6 25	..	..	9*30	..	11*15	..
Clapham	..	..	6 35	..	..	9*40	..	11*25	..
Newby..................	..	..	6 40	..	..	9*45	..	11*30	..
Ingleton (Ingleboro. Htl. arr.	..	..	6 55	..	..	10*0	..	11*45	..
Ingleton do. dep.	..	..	7 0	..	..	..	..	..	..
Burton-in-Lonsdale	..	..	7 10	..	..	..	..	..	..
Cantsfield	..	..	7 20	..	..	..	..	..	..
Melling	..	..	7 30	..	..	..	..	..	..
Hornby	..	..	7 37	..	..	..	..	..	..
Claughton	..	..	7 45	..	..	..	..	..	..
Caton	..	..	7 55	..	..	..	..	..	..
Lancaster (Dalton Sq.)	..	..	8 10	..	..	..	..	..	..
Morecambe ....arr.	..	..	8 30	..	..	..	..	..	..

* Saturday Only.

SKIPTON TO SETTLE, INGLETON & MORECAMBE.

SUNDAYS.

(Town Hall)	A.M.	A.M.	P.M.	P.M.	P.M.	P.M.	P.M.	P.M.	P.M.	P.M.	P.M.	P.M.
Skipton ....dep.	9 40	1145	1 0	2 0	2 30	3 45	5 10	6 10	6 45	8 0	9 0	10 0
Gargrave	9 55	12 0	1 15	2 15	2 45	4 0	5 25	6 25	7 0	8 15	9 15	1015
Conistone Cold	10 0	12 7	1 22	2 22	2 52	4 7	5 32	6 32	7 7	8 22	9 22	1022
Hellifield.............	1010	1222	1 37	2 37	3 7	4 22	5 47	6 47	7 17	8 37	9 32	1037
Long Preston	1017	1230	1 45	2 45	3 15	4 30	5 55	6 55	7 25	8 45	9 40	1045
Settle (Market Place) arr.	1030	1245	2 0	3 0	3 30	4 45	6 10	7 10	7 40	9 0	9 55	11 0
Settle (Market Plce) dep.	1030	..	..	3 0	..	..	..	7 10	..	..	..	..
Austwick	1045	..	..	3 15	..	..	..	7 25	..	..	..	..
Clapham	1050	..	..	3 25	..	..	..	7 35	..	..	..	..
Newby...............	1055	..	..	3 30	..	..	..	7 40	..	..	..	..
Ingleton (Ingleb. Htl) arr	1110	..	..	3 50	..	..	..	7 55	..	..	..	..
Ingleton Do. dep.	1110	..	..	4 0	..	..	..	..	..	..	..	..
Burton-in-Lonsdale	1120	..	..	4 10	..	..	..	..	..	..	..	..
Cantsfield	1130	..	..	4 20	..	..	..	..	..	..	..	..
Melling	1140	..	..	4 30	..	..	..	..	..	..	..	..
Hornby	1147	..	..	4 37	..	..	..	..	..	..	..	..
Claughton	1155	..	..	4 45	..	..	..	..	..	..	..	..
Caton	12 5	..	..	4 55	..	..	..	..	..	..	..	..
Lancaster (Dalton Sq.)	1220	..	..	5 10	..	..	..	..	..	..	..	..
Morecambe........ arr.	1240	..	..	5 30	..	..	..	..	..	..	..	..

Pennine Motors.

Time Tables

For WINTER SEASON 1928-29,

Commencing Monday, Oct. 22nd, 1928, until further notice,

Between Skipton, Gargrave, Hellifield, Settle, Ingleton, Tosside, & Wigglesworth, Burton-in-Lonsdale, Lancaster and Morecambe.

Large and Small Parties Specially Catered For.

HEADQUARTERS :—

Pennine Garage, Gargrave. Tel. 15.

Albion Garage, Skipton.

"Craven Herald" Works, Skipton. Tel. 191.

SKIPTON to GARGRAVE.

WEEKDAYS.

Skipton (Town Hall), dep.—6-30 a.m., 7-10, 7-45, 9-0, 10-25 11-30, 12-40, 1-15, 2-25, 3-0, 3-25, 4-30, 5-10, 5-35, 6-20 7-5, 8-0 9-5, 10-0.

Gargrave (The Square), dep.—7-10 a.m., 8-10, 8-15, 9-25, 10-55, 12-10, 1-40, 2-20, 3-0, 4-10 5-10, 5-55, 6-25, 7-5, 7-30, 8-25, 9-40, 10-50.

SATURDAYS.

Skipton (Town Hall), dep.—6-30 a.m., 7-10, 7-45, 9-0, 10-25, 11-30, 12-25, 12-40, 1-0, 1-15, 1-40, 2-25, 3-0, 3-25. 4-0, 4-30, 4-50, 5-10, 5-35, 6-0, 6-5, 6-20, 6-35, 7-0, 7-5, 7-45, 8-0, 8-45, 9-0, 9-5, 9-30, 10-0, 10-40, 11-5, 11-10.

Gargrave (The Square), dep.—7-10 a.m., 8-10, 8-15, 9-25, 10-55 12-10, 12-40, 1-20, 1-40, 2-0, 2-25, 3-0, 3-30, 4-10 4-30, 5-10, 5-50, 5-55, 6-15, 6-25, 6-50, 7-5, 7-25, 8-0, 8-25, 8-45, 9-0, 9-15, 9-40, 9-45, 10-15, 11-50, 12-40.

SUNDAYS.

Skipton (Town Hall), dep.—9-40 a.m., 10-10, 11-45, 1-0 p.m., 2-0, 2-30, 3-45, 5-10, 6-10, 6-45. 7-30, 8-0, 8-30, 9-0, 10-0.

Gargrave (The Square), dep.—9-45 a.m., 10-40, 12-40 p.m., 1-55 2-55, 4-20, 5-25, 6-0, 6-40 7-30, 8-0, 8-25, 9-0, 9-25, 10-40.

Morecambe, Ingleton, Settle, Skipton.

WEEKDAYS.

	A.M.	A.M.	A.M.	A.M.	A.M.	P.M.	P.M.	P.M.	P.M.
Morecambe ....dep.	..	..	..	..	..	..	..	..	1245
Lancaster (Dalton Sq.)	..	..	..	..	..	..	..	..	1 5
Caton	..	..	..	..	..	..	..	..	1 20
Claughton	..	..	.	..	..	..	..	..	1 30
Hornby	..	..	..	..	..	..	..	..	1 38
Melling	..	..	..	..	..	..	..	..	1 45
Cantsfield	..	..	..	..	..	..	..	..	1 55
Burton-in-Lonsdale	..	..	..	..	..	..	..	..	2 5
Ingleton (Ingleb. Hotel) arr.	..	..	..	..	..	..	..	..	2 20
Ingleton do. dep.	..	..	8 0	9 30	1045	..	..	..	2 35
Newby..	..	..	8 10	9 40	1055	..	..	..	2 50
Clapham	..	..	8 15	9 45	11 0	..	..	..	2 55
Austwick	..	..	8 25	9 55	1110	..	..	..	3 5
Settle (Market Place) .. arr.	..	..	8 45	1015	1130	..	..	..	3 30
Settle Do. dep.	6 30	7 30	8 45	1015	1130	1 0	1*45	2 20	3 30
Long Preston	6 45	7 45	9 0	1030	1145	1 15	2* 0	2 35	3 45
Hellifield................	6 52	7 52	9 7	1037	1152	1 22	2* 7	2 42	3 52
Conistone Cold	7 2	8 2	9 17	1047	12 2	1 32	2*17	2 52	4 2
Gargrave	7 10	8 10	9 25	1055	1210	1 40	2*25	3 0	4 10
Skipton ....arr.	7 25	8 25	9 45	1115	1230	2 0	2*45	3 20	4 30

* Saturdays Only.

MORECAMBE TO INGLETON, SETTLE AND SKIPTON.

WEEKDAYS.—Continued.

	P.M.	P.M.	P.M.	P.M.	P.M.	P.M.	P.M.	P.M.	P.M.	P.M.
Morecambe ......dep.	..	..	..	..	5 15	..	..	..	8 45	..
Lancaster (Dalton Sq.)	..	..	..	..	5 35	..	..	..	9 5	..
Caton	..	..	..	..	5 50	..	..	..	9 20	..
Claughton.............	..	..	..	..	6 0	..	..	..	9 30	..
Hornby	..	..	..	..	6 8	..	..	..	9 38	..
Melling	..	..	..	..	6 15	..	..	..	9 45	..
Cantsfield	..	..	..	..	6 25	..	..	..	9 55	..
Burton-in-Lonsdale ..	..	..	..	..	6 35	..	..	..	10 5	..
Ingleton (Ingleb. Hl. arr	..	..	..	..	6 50	..	..	..	1015	..
Ingleton Do. dep.	..	4 20	..	..	7 0	..	..	..	10*15	11*45
Newby	..	4 35	..	..	7 10	..	..	..	10*20	11*55
Clapham	..	4 40	..	..	7 15	..	..	..	10*25	12* 0
Austwick	..	4 50	..	..	7 25	..	..	..	10*35	..
Settle (Mkt. Place) arr.	..	5 15	..	..	7 45	..	..	..	10*55	12*30
Settle Do. dep.	4 30	5 15	5 45	6 25	7 45	8* 5	9 0	1010	11*10	12* 0
Long Preston	4 45	5 30	6 0	6 40	8 0	8*20	9 15	1025	11*25	12*15
Hellifield	4 52	5 37	6 7	6 47	8 7	8*27	9 22	1032	11*32	12*22
Conistone Cold	5 2	5 47	6 17	6 57	8 17	8*37	9 32	1042	11*42	12*32
Gargrave	5 10	5 55	6 25	7 5	8 25	8*45	9 40	1050	11*50	12*40
Skipton .... arr.	5 30	6 15	6 45	7 25	8 45	9* 5	10 0	1110	12*10	1* 0

MORECAMBE TO INGLETON, SETTLE & SKIPTON.

SUNDAYS.

	A.M.	A.M.	P.M.	P.M.	P.M.	P.M.	P.M.	P.M.	P.M.	P.M.	P.M.	P.M
Morecambe........dep.	..	..	..	..	..	2 25	..	..	..	6 25	..	..
Lancaster	..	..	..	..	..	2 45	..	..	..	6 45	..	..
Caton	..	..	..	..	..	3 0	..	..	..	7 0	..	..
Claughton	..	..	..	..	..	3 10	..	..	..	7 10	..	..
Hornby	..	..	..	..	..	3 18	..	..	..	7 18	..	..
Melling	..	..	..	..	..	3 25	..	..	..	7 25	..	..
Cantsfield	..	..	..	..	..	3 35	..	..	..	7 35	..	..
Burton-in-Lonsdale	..	..	..	..	..	3 45	..	..	..	7 45	..	..
Ingleton (Ingleb Htl) arr	..	..	..	..	..	3 55	..	..	..	7 55	..	..
Ingleton Do. dep.	..	1120	..	..	..	4 0	..	..	..	8 0	..	..
Newby...............	..	1130	..	..	..	4 10	..	..	..	8 10	..	..
Clapham	..	1135	..	..	..	4 15	..	..	..	8 15	..	..
Austwick	..	1140	..	..	..	4 25	..	..	..	8 25	..	..
Settle (Market Place) arr.	..	12 0	..	..	..	4 45	..	..	..	8 45	..	..
Settle Do. dep.	10 0	12 0	1 15	2 15	3 40	4 45	6 0	6 50	7 45	8 45	10 0	..
Long Preston	1015	1215	1 30	2 30	3 55	5 0	6 15	7 5	8 0	9 0	1015	..
Hellifield.............	1022	1222	1 37	2 37	4 0	5 7	6 22	7 12	8 7	9 7	1022	..
Conistone Cold	1032	1232	1 47	2 47	4 12	5 17	6 32	7 22	8 17	9 17	1032	..
Gargrave	1040	1240	1 55	2 55	4 20	5 25	6 40	7 30	8 25	9 25	1040	..
Skipton ....arr.	11 0	1 0	2 15	3 15	4 40	5 45	7 0	7 50	8 45	9 45	11 0	..

LONG PRESTON, WIGGLESWORTH, TOSSIDE.

TUESDAY ONLY.

	A.M.		P.M.
Long Preston. .dep.	1030	Tosside... ....dep.	4 20
Wigglesworth	1040	Wigglesworth	4 30
Tosside ...... arr.	1045	Long Preston .. arr.	4 45

TOSSIDE, WIGGLESWORTH, RATHMELL, SETTLE.

TUESDAY ONLY.

	A.M.	P.M.	P.M.
Tosside ....dep.	10 45	..	..
Wigglesworth	10 55	1 45	3.00
Rathmell	11 5	1 55	3.10
Settle.....................arr.	11 20		3.25

	P.M.	P.M.	p.m
Settle ....dep.	1 15	2 30	3 45
Rathmell	1 30	2 45	3 55
Wigglesworth	1 40	2 55	4 5
Tosside ....arr.	..	..	4 20

ALL PARCELS MUST BE CARRIAGE PAID.

Pennine Garage .. Gargrave. Tel. 15.
" " .. Albion Square, Skipton.

Return Tickets are available for 3 months from date of issue.

To the TRAVELLING PUBLIC.

In your Interests

SUPPORT LOCAL AND PRIVATE ENTERPRISE

We Guarantee that

Existing

Cheap Fares Will be Retained

But only by Travelling by

The Pennine Service

The Pioneers of the Skipton--Settle 'Bus Route (owned solely by Ex-Service Men).

Hand-bill issued by Pennine in the early years.
Pennine collection

SKIPTON URBAN DISTRICT COUNCIL.

ALLOCATION OF BUS STANDS BY THE COUNCIL.

Town Hall Front. Stand for 4 buses.

1.	Wharfedale Bus Co.	1 stand for	Wharfe Valley District.
2.	Pennine Bus Co.	1 " "	Gargrave Road and the North
3.	Ribble Bus Co.	1 " "	Gargrave Road and the North,
4.	Do. Do.	1 " "	Embsay.

Note:- Buses on the Town Hall front must keep within the line of studs so as to leave clear the road leading to the Cattle Market.

Free Library Front. Stand for 2 buses.

1	West Yorks. Co.	1 stand for Ilkley.
2.	Do. Do.	1 stand for Grassington and District.

Caroline Square. Stand for 7 buses.

1.	Messrs Laycock	1 stand for	Earby and Colne.
2.	" "	1 " "	Barnoldswick
3.	Ribble Bus Co,	1 " "	Blackburn
4.	Do. Do.	1 " "	Colne.
5.	Silver Star	2 stands for	Carleton, Bradley and Broughton Road.
6.	Cononley Motors.	1 stand for	Cononley.

Note.:- The buses on this stand must keep behind the line of studs in order not to block the end of Newmarket St.

Sackville Street.

1.	West Yorks.Co.	3 stand for Keighley, Bradford and Silsden.

The stands are not be used by buses as waiting rooms No bus is to be on the stand longer than 15 mins. before starting time.

Companies are to keep to the stands allotted to them.

A copy of the plan shewing the stands will be supplied to each company.

Surveyor. ....

Supt. of Police..........................

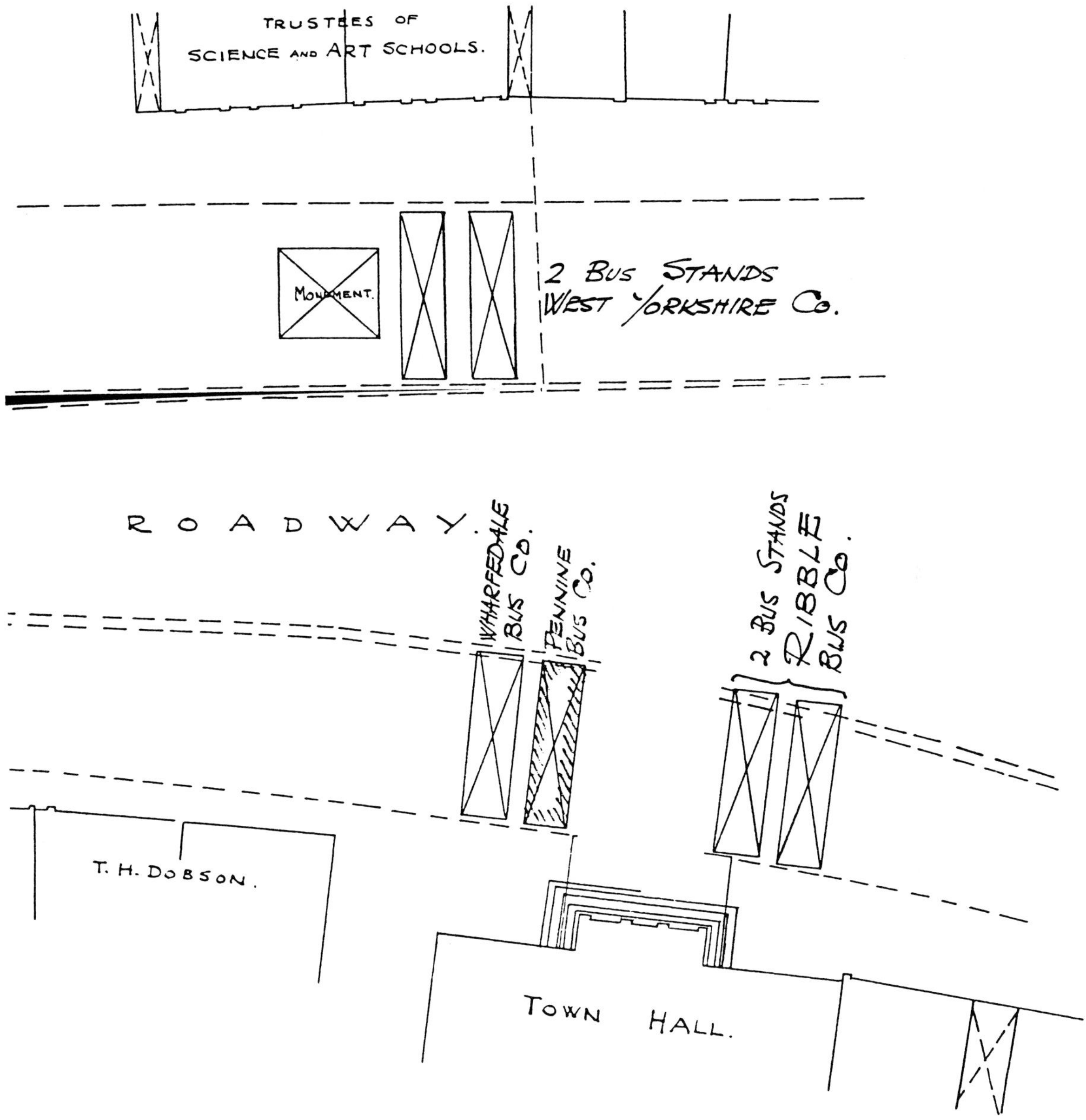

The letter on the opposite page was dated May 1930 and was sent out by Skipton Urban District Council to bus companies using Skipton High Street as a departure point. Along with the above plan it indicated the allocation of stands for the respective companies. Re- Sackville Street. Interestingly the West Yorkshire Road Car Company had 3 stands there for services into South Craven and no stands in Caroline Square. Sometime in the next decade West Yorkshire services were transfered into Caroline Square, and after the War, and up to the opening of Skipton Bus Station, Ribble moved onto Sackville Street. Pennine collection

Leyland Lion WX 3736 was new in 1930 and was photographed at Ingleton on 7 June that year working the Morecambe - Skipton service.
Pennine collection

The subject of early Pennine bus liveries is interesting. We know that probably all three of the Overland buses were painted blue and for later buses Pennine adopted a livery of all-over maroon nicely lined out in (gold?). The Company name was applied in gold leaf. The livery was then changed to orange lower panels with black upper panels and roof, seperated by a duck-egg blue stripe. It is confirmed by Norman Simpson that this change came about following a visit made by the partners to Leyland to take delivery of their(then)latest *Lioness* (in that case it would be 1927), where they noticed Leyland's own coach being painted in its football team colours of orange and black with a grey stripe. This colour scheme was immediately liked and the partners thought it would make an excellent livery and enable passengers and others to recognise a Pennine bus when they saw one.

This Lion WX 2979 was new in 1930 and had a Leyland body. It was almost certainly the first new Pennine bus to receive the orange, black and duck-egg blue stripe livery. Note the speed limit was then 20mph. When photographed it was brand new and unregistered.
Pennine collection

A rear view of WX 2979 when new. Note the Hackney Carriage 30 seats plate. Of particular interest is the livery, interestingly the orange panels are lined in gold - a relic from the maroon livery! How long the gold lining continued to be applied on orange is not known. Pennine collection

Accordingly the earlier all-over maroon livery was phased out in favour of the new colours. At this point the picture becomes unclear. The partners may have liked this livery when they saw Leyland's own coach(1927), but it must have been well into the 1930s before orange, grey and duck-egg blue was applied to all the fleet. Until the 1950s the Company's name was applied in gold leaf, but plastic transfers are now used.

An article in the November 1963 *Passenger Transport* magazine states that in 1927 "the partners acquired their first Leyland - and the present Pennine livery of orange and black. Taking delivery of this first Leyland, a *Leveret* , Mr A.D.Simpson went across to Lancashire and saw an attractive bus in these colours belonging to the Leyland football team. Previously the Pennine livery had been maroon, but permission was readily given to have the new bus painted in the orange and black livery". This implies that the *Leveret* was the first vehicle to be painted in orange, black and duck-egg blue but unfortunately we do not have a photograph to confirm or otherwise. Certainly new Leylands delivered after the *Leveret* were in maroon livery.

Unfortunately we do not have photographs for all the early fleet but most of those seen and reproduced in this Chapter show an overall livery which is lined out. This surely must be maroon. Without being able to prove it conclusively we think the position was as follows:

From the Pennine list and perusal of photographs it seems that the 3 Overlands started life blue and one was repainted orange. it seems probable that following the Overlands all vehicles from WU 8434 to WX 3736 of 1930 except WX 2979 or WX 3735 were painted maroon and lined out. One of the last two mentioned would have been the first orange, black and duck-egg blue Pennine bus. A photo of a 1930 *Lion* in the new livery was published in *Buses Illustrated* for March 1964 and WX 2979 seems to be the likely candidate. WX 3735 would probably be the last bus painted maroon when new. Starting with the AEC coach in 1931 all vehicles were either turned out new or eventually repainted in orange, black and duck-egg blue. It seems quite probably that the first orange re-paint would have been Overland WU 4197. Over the years grey has replaced the duck-egg blue, but orange, grey and black are still the official livery colours. There have of course been exceptions to the rule with a few vehicles in a coaching livery of all-over cream with orange flairs, wings and mud-guards. This livery was introduced in 1949 on HYG 60, a 33-seat coach with Wilks & Meade body. After the second World War WW 9817, one of the 1929 *Tigers,* was rebodied with a coach body but appears to have been painted orange with no cream flairs.

An earlier livery exception was a pair of AEC single-deck buses purchased just after the Second World War from Halifax Corporation - these operated in Halifax colours with the Halifax orange looking positively anaemic when compared to the rich Pennine orange.

There remains one orange and cream liveried coach to this day, used on excursion and school trip work.

Registration No.	New	Make	Notes
WU 4197†	1925	Overland	Originally blue - WU 4197 - the last Overland is documented as being “the one eventually painted orange”.
WU 3749	1925	Overland	Originally blue.
WU 6162	1926	Overland	Originally blue.
WU 8434	1926	Leyland Leveret	No photograph seen.
WW 154	1927	Leyland Lioness	No photograph seen.
WW 1174	1927	Leyland Lioness	Photograph - maroon - lined out when new.
WW 3322	1927	Star Flyer	Photograph - maroon - lined out when new.
WW 5185	1928	Leyland Lion	Photograph - maroon - lined out when new.
WW 5186	1928	Leyland Lion	No photograph seen.
WW 9531	1929	Leyland Tiger	Photograph 1930s - maroon - lined out when new.
WW 9817*	1929	Leyland Tiger	Photograph 1930s - maroon - lined out when new.
WW 9818	1929	Leyland Tiger	Photograph 1930s - maroon - lined out when new.
WX 2979	1930	Leyland Lion	Photograph 1930 - orange, black, duck-egg blue stripe when new.
WX 3735	1930	Leyland Lion	No photograph seen when new.
WX 3736	1930	Leyland Lion	Photograph 1930s - maroon - lined out when new.
WX 7431	1931	AEC Regal	Photograph - orange, black, duck-egg blue stripe when new.
AWX 763	1935	Leyland Tiger	Photograph - orange, black, duck-egg blue stripe when new.
AWX 764	1935	Leyland Tiger	Photograph - orange, black, duck-egg blue stripe when new.
WU 9999	1927	Dennis ‘E’	Ex-Hull 1927.
YG 3405	1932	Lance 1	Ex-Parker 1935.
CK 4295	1930	Leyland Tiger	Ex-Ribble 1938. Photograph - orange, black, duck-egg stripe in 1938.
CK 4296	1930	Leyland Tiger	Ex-Ribble 1938. Photograph - orange, black, duck-egg stripe in 1938.
CK 4297	1930	Leyland Tiger	Ex-Ribble 1938. Photograph - orange, black, duck-egg stripe in 1938.

† This bus was actually the first in service but may have been the last of the type to run. May have been WU 4097.
* When fitted with coach body the livery was all orange - no cream flash.

The bus stands at the bottom of Skipton High Street with Ribble Pennine and Keighley West Yorkshire buses in view. The Pennine vehicle is ex-Ribble CK 4297 one of a batch purchased second-hand in 1938. Note the luggage rack. The date was June 1943 - note the white edges to the mudguards and the blacked out head lamps with only a slit.

An official photograph of AEC Regal 1 coach WX 7431. Tony Edwards collection

WX 7431 was built as an AEC Regal 1 with a 32 seat rear entrance coach body by Burlingham , entering service in 1931. The indicator shows 'Pennine' at one side and 'Special' at the other. The livery is orange and black with a duck-egg blue stripe - one of the first Pennine buses so painted. It was photographed with its driver Harry Addyman, conductor, and other officials. Next to the driver is A.D.Simpson Pennine collection

AWX 764 was the second 1936 Tiger and was photographed at the present Skipton Bus Station in the early 1950s before it received a second-hand coach body off WW 9817. Both AWX 763 and AWX 764 were used as ambulances during the War years, working from Wakefield. When sold, this vehicle did not stray far from Pennine territory, going to Hillcrest Coaches, Ingleton.
The late R.F.Mack Tony Edwards collection

In 1936 a pair of Leyland Tiger TS7 buses were purchased new and one AWX 763 is shown climbing Buckhaw Brow(near Giggleswick) on the main Settle-Kendal road, bound for Ingleton. A 1929 or 1930 Tiger or Lion is preparing to descend - one of the few photographs showing this type in orange, black and duck-egg blue livery.
Pennine collection

The reminiscences and notes which make up this Chapter are all from Pennine records and have been provided by Mr Norman Simpson , Partner in Pennine Motor Services and show some of the problems encountered in running a Dales bus company in the pre-second World War period.

It would be impossible to mention all those who have worked for Pennine throughout the 75 years of operation but certain members of staff should be mentioned.

Henry Fletcher was the first driver to join Pennine receiving £2.50 per week in 1926 and he moved to South Street, Gargrave on his marriage and was to stay with the Company for the rest of his working life becoming the coach driver later on.

Other old timers included Lionel Thornton, a driver who stayed with Pennine for life and continued as a Conductor in his old age. A fussy man he politely helped passengers off his bus until one day he took too long and the Driver drove off and left him.

Harold Dryden joined Pennine in 1928 as a Conductor later becoming an Inspector continuing to work past retirement age in the office at Gargrave, retiring in 1983 and passing away six years later. A mild quiet man with great strength of character he arrived in Lancaster one day from Skipton where he had 30 minute lunch break. He promptly went to the dentist and had all his teeth out and at 12.50pm conducted his bus home! These were men of guts. Harold's wife Alice was a Conductress at Settle.

Ernest Collins was another stalwart having served in the 1914-18 War and later with the Black & Tans in Ireland. After the War he went home to Norfolk and replied to an advert for a motor mechanic at Grouse Garage. So when Pennine purchased the garage he came with it. After retirement age Ernest continued to work for seven years as a fitter and weekend driver between Skipton and Gargrave, staying at the wheel until he was 72 years old. That give him 7 extra years pension contributions at the rate of an extra 6d per year on his pension making 3/6 extra for those 7 years. He then worked part time for two years until May 1965 when aged 74 he went back to Norfolk, re-married and took on deliveries for the local butcher until his 90s.

Another old employee was Walter Bates. Before joining Pennine he had been coachman to a vet and had also driven a steam lorry in Manchester - this had solid wheels with cast iron brakes. A man of great strength he had pulled out a 15 ton bog oak with a team of horses and loaded them on his own. Known affectionately as Watty, one day whilst crossing Clapham Common with LWY 702 he crashed into a milk tanker because neither would give way. Remarkably he was still driving the school bus in his late 70s. He had a bump on Airton bridge and the Insurance Company declined further cover. He retired in 1960 and worked until June 1968 passing away in the following year.

The Addyman family were also Pennine employees with David, a man of immense strength, responsible for starting the buses by the time-honoured starting handle method and responsible for fueling the buses. Harry Addyman was one of the first Drivers. Jack was a joiner with the Skipton Castle Estate before joining Pennine becoming responsible for re-building the buses after the War.

In more recent years mention should be made of Peter Beckwith, the Grouse Garage mechanic who clocked up some 50 years service. Also the present Company Secretary Roger Wheatstone with 32 years service without whose help Norman Simpson admits he could not have managed.

In the early years Arthur Hull's Gargrave service started from the Old George Hotel, in Skipton. Wharfedale Motors services started on the frontage of Skipton Town Hall as did those of Pennine, Old Bill Motors(who ran a good service to Embsay), and later the West Yorkshire Road Car Co., who were quite ruthless in their behaviour in front of the Town Hall. Another early bus operator was Nicholas Smith(of haulage fame)who had a route from Skipton to Keighley. Another early pioneer was John Hey, he ran to Carleton and used to buy his oil from Simpson Brothers.

The Town Hall front was by now overcrowded and Pennine decided to alter its starting point to the Penny Bank(later Yorkshire Bank), using this frontage for several years until the bus station was built in 1950. Before 1950 a few bus companies started from Caroline Square at the bottom of the High Street, including Ezra Laycock - later to be bought out by Pennine. Ribble started on Sackville Street opposite the Plaza Cinema.

The garage yard at Gargrave was immediately behind the Grouse Hotel. Some of the buses purchased from Ribble had ladders up the back so buses were strategically parked beneath the bar-maids window. This was certainly of great benefit to the ladies friends!.

Early buses were only of low capacity and at peak times it was not uncommon in order to avoid the crush, for small children to ride with the driver, sitting on the wheel arch next to him watching him manipulate the gears as the world flashed by. Heads had to be kept down and no interference in any way with the driver. Cab floors were single-skinned with gaps around the pedals, hand-brake and gear lever, so floors were packed solid with newspapers to stop a gale entering the cab through the floor. The early buses had single-skin roofs and in winter the breath of the passengers froze on the roof making the most fantastic patterns. One Clayton Dewandre coil heater was fitted behind the engine and proved absolutely useless especially when the Conductor stood infront of it - hence the issue of overcoats. It was possible on the early vehicles to wipe the windscreen manually when the wipers were not functioning correctly.

There are always delays on the roads because of accidents and other problems. Yesteryear, numerous flocks of sheep and cattle were regularly driven into Skipton Auction adjacent to the railway, for movement south. Flocks of sheep up to 500 at a time, could be seen, one flock behind the other - purgatory for the driver going the same way but not so dificult if you were facing them. The Pennine bus driver was always helped if possible because the drovers were allowed to travel free - the only customers trusted with this privelege, for until the drove was completed the drovers were not paid. They were poor but extremely honest.

While mentioning sheep it is appropriate to mention sheeps(cats)eyes - the invention of a Mr Shaw - reflecting studs set in the road. With poor headlights and fog in winter the drivers thought these 'cats eyes' were wonderful. In the earlier years the drivers were for the time very highly paid and needed to be with crash gears, indifferent brakes, no heating and no de-misting. The answer to misting up was half an apple wiped on the inside of the windscreen. Neither was there the luxury of electric starters - it was a case of swinging the engine to start and lot of men lost teeth, broke ribs and arms when the engine was not sufficiently retarded - a match box was just the right size to insert in the ignition to retard it.

One day Blackey a dealer from Malham accidently left a packet of money wrapped in newspaper on the luggage rack of a Pennine bus and one week later he enquired it if had been found. A search then discovered the parcel of money on the rack exactly where it had been left and the dealer was asked to call and collect it. As he was ready to leave the office he was asked if he had forgotten something so he apologised profuseley and departed in a .... great hurry with his £300 without offering a reward.

Passing through Long Preston a new driver saw his friend waving at him and waved back. However his friend was wanting the bus to stop. The bus did not stop so he complained - a small misunderstanding.

During the 1914-18 War Joe Hargreaves was in the Grenadier Guards and was very badly gassed, suffering badly for the rest of his life with lungs that were shot at. A Pennine driver, he later became an Inspector but was transferred to mechanic duties. Whilst on the service to Morecambe he sat on the front all day and returned home at midnight with no passengers arriving back at Skipton. Suddenly Joe remembered he has left his box with the cash in at the Morecambe turn round so promptly drove back to Morecambe where his box was still under the seat. He quickly returned with his box ready to start out again at 6.30am. Joe became an Inspector but was quickly transferred to the garage when he was heard explaining it was the best job he had ever had - ride to Morecambe every morning, listen to the band all day and return home in the evening. As a mechanic he made a big mistake when he tried to remove a front wheel without jacking the bus up. He was trapped by the arms and dare not move so he shouted for help. Unfortunately he was ignored for some time because the other mechanics thought he was shouting to tell them it was lunch break ...

Taffy Philips returning from Tosside one day had to travel through floodwater at Rathmel. This was so deep that the passengers sat on the seat backs and had to open the rear emergency door to let the water through as it was building up inside. Taffy put his feet on the dash and a jack handle on the throttle. Sadly there was a hole for the starting handle which forced water into the engine, this coming out of the oil filler at the top of the engine. He was towed home.

Whilst the cutting was being made between Coniston and Hellifield drivers used to take fish and chips to the night watchman who had a small hut and brazier, Vic, late one night accidently caught the hut and tipped it and the night watchman into the hole.

Interestingly Pennine records show that double-decker buses would have been used on the Skipton - Settle route, but for the fact that the Skew Bridge at Settle would not allow them owing to height.

Nothing on any vehicle is more important than brakes, even when the old horse vehicles were in use and the brake shoes were mens shoes fastened onto the brake pads. These did the trick in those days, but now, as buses and coaches get heavier and carry greater weights and are for ever faster, something more substantial is required. Our early Overlands had good brakes, apart

An early Pennine bus which was probably the normal control Leyland Leveret WU 8434, a 20 seater added to the fleet in 1926. From left to right, Henry Fletcher, A .V .Simpson, Ernest Collings & Joe Hargreaves.
Pennine Collection

from having internal brakes, there were external brakes lapped completely round the drum, and being efficient, they had a long life. The Leyland early brakes were not too good, the *Leveret* brakes grated a lot, particularly if it had been raining. This machine had a brake on the propellor shaft, which gave a lot of trouble. Rear brake drums were fitted but caused much worry. The next, Leyland *Lioness* had good brakes even so they could have been better, for the *Lioness* was prone to brake grabbing so a different brake lining was used to stop this, it was called 'Ferrobestos'. This was fitted to the leading shoe and the trailing shoe did all the braking. This was a cause of drums cracking. It follows that if one shoe in each drum does all the work, great heat is generated. Radiators behaved well, but it would be a good petrol engine that could go 50,000 without valves grinding and decoking. Starters, dynamo and pumps were for ever giving trouble. Salt also played the devil with bus bodies. Tyres have improved.

One of the early buses had the exhaust routed through the saloon for heating, a good idea until the fumes escaped. It was quickly rerouted under the bus.

Silencers were always a problem, the early ones were up to six feet long so on one model a piston was driven into the back end of the silencer to seal it. This did the trick until one day going down into Coniston Cold the engine back-fired and blew it out rickocheting under the vehicle, the noise was impressive the driver stopped at the bus stop, rang the garage having just picked up a red hot piston off the road, and announced the engine had collapsed and was coming out of the exhaust. The first diesel powered buses were stopped by pulling the accelerator back.

As with any industry the correct insurance is a must. Pennine's insurance agents' have always been Harold Connew & Son Ltd, Leeds. Their original insurers were the British Standard Assurance Association, later changed to Premier Motor Policies before becoming part of Eagle Star. In the earlier days accidents were frequent even though speeds were low and there was less traffic on the roads, and 31 claims were made against insurance between March 1928 and September 1929.

The accident reports from those earlier days make interesting reading. But they are inspirational. "As I was passing the lamp post it leaned out and hit the bus", "I was overtaken by a galloping horse and cart, the cart-wheel hit the bus" - and so on.

On 27 May 1932 an accident occurred at the Skipton High Street bus stand outside the Yorkshire Bank when a child from Coniston Cold reputedly had his legs crushed above the knees. The bus driver was C.Wilson, his speed 2mph, conditions wet. In the accident report the driver stated that he was pulling up to the bus stand and as it was raining heavily the intending passengers made a rush for the bus door and young Master Alan Seed was apparently pushed under the near-side front wheel. He was conveyed to Gargrave at his own request by private car to Doctor Wales and then forward to his home. The claim was not persued by the passenger. Nor did Pennine make a counter-claim for damage to their bus!

A report dated 23 June 1931 involved WW 5185, driver Packham and conductor Harold Dryden with Mr Yeoman of Ribble witnessing the event. The Pennine driver stated that whilst proceeding up Skirbeck Hill to Skipton, a steam roller belonging to the West Yorkshire County Council was repairing the road. As the bus approached the engine, it appeared to jump side-ways onto the mudguard. The front of the bus passed the roller and no impact was felt. Mr Yeoman, who was a passenger, requested the driver to inspect the bus when they arrived in Skipton where he found the mud-guard badly torn. Weather conditions were good and the speed was 12mph.

Driver Wilfred Wilson, Conductor W.Staveley, *Lion* WW 5186, 17 February 1931."Whilst proceeding from Caton to Lancaster, a schoolboy, Master Meadowcroft, fell out of the bus through the rear emergency door for some reason unbenown to us, and burst his nose. The speed was between 15 and 20mph".

Walter Bates 29 March 1933 *Lion* WX 2979. "Whilst proceeding from Long Preston to Hellifield a vehicle infront turned causing him to veer into the offside of the road scraping a signpost. On reaching the third party for an explanation of his action, our driver found the driver concerned in the accident had changed seats with the authorised driver. Subsequently it was proved that the driver concerned had no licence".

Driver Walter Bates 5 January 1940. Conductor Earl Capstick. Speed 25mph. Weather fine. Roads icebound. Police. P.C.Lofthouse, Hellifield(This was War-time and headlights were covered except for slit)"I was driving the 6.30am bus from Settle to Skipton. At 6.55am I pulled into the rear side because a lorry was approaching and on getting level with the lorry. I noticed a postman on a bicycle about three yards infront of me with no lights on. I swerved to avoid a collision with him and went through the wall on the off side of the road. Damage - both front springs broken. Windows, panels and wings broken and damaged. Dropped four feet into a field, drove out through the gate, subsequently found front axle bent. Injuries - cuts, bruises and shock to four passengers - No claims".

'No claims' was typical of that period and totally different to the present time when the general attitude is 'how much can we get'. The present enthusiasm to sue for damages is shown by a communication from Solicitors re-'a supposed accident' to a passengers foot. Fortunately in this modern age of computers, the policeman who had sent for the ambulance was traced and he had talked to the ambulance crew who told the Constable that it was the second time that night they had taken the plaintiff to hospital for his foot. Thereafter was a sudden silence from his Solicitors.

The driver was very quick witted when a drunk boarded the bus at Settle for Skipton. The customer was swearing and most objectionable so at Hellifield the driver announced "Skipton" the drunk alighted and the bus drove off and left him.

Pennine also had an oil reclaiming machine to heat the oil and force through filters under pressure. This was in the days of straight oil. Arthur Simpson showed it to Jim Windle but forgot the pressure was on. He took the top off and Uncle Jim was drowned in oil. Sure he had done it on purpose! There was a time when for a number of years the two would not speak to each other except through H.Dryden or H.Fletcher. But they got over it. This was due to Arthur Simpson going off for a few years to build his own house and Jim Windle going off to work for County Motors - a motor car garage. Father was the only one who stayed at work for Pennine and was totally loyal, honest and committed to Pennine with a great grasp of financial matters. There was a feeling amongst the Partners that not all were pulling their weight. Arthur complained about Jim and Jim hit back about the house.

We still have a lathe by Smith Barker Wilson, of Halifax also chucks and gears for screw cutting. Arthur Simpson sold a souvenir revolver, for £14 to buy the lathe at the end of the War and it is still used.

Oxy-acetelene welding was also a great tool in the early days and helped particularly during the second War to keep the buses on the road. One day Arthur Windle berated Jimmy Crook for taking too long to paint the ceiling white in one bus and announced he would show him how to do it. Afterwards, Jimmy told him if he had used the sweeping brush he could have done it twice as quick, the result was such a mess. Arthur was not pleased and took his leave before normality returned.

Pennine provided a country bus service of immediate appeal to villagers who were then able to day-trip from their villages and farms. The big advantage was that the bus stopped at the door and was handy - unlike the railway whose stations were seldom near to a town or village centre.

Drivers wore blue overcoats in winter and long white coats in the summer. Initially the driver also served as the conductor and tickets were only given for return journeys. There was not time to bother issuing single tickets, the customers paid and the fare was dropped into the bag. The fare from Skipton to Gargrave was 5d and 8d return, though before 9am when workers were moving, the fare was 6d return. There were no official bus stops and the bus stopped anywhere it was required to. Not only human passengers were carried, but Pennine conveyed farm products and animals; sheep, calfs, goats and general parcels. A farmer might leave a calf covered in sacking and this would be laid at the back of the bus near the emergency door. If a sheep had to be transported it would be tethered to one of the legs of a back seat. The person who left it would give instructions as to which farm it should be left at. Often, drivers were asked to collect a prescription at the doctors' surgery and then to go to the chemists' to have the prescription made up and drop it off on the return journey. A Skipton chemist, Illingworth's had a traveller who went as far as Bentham and the villages inbetween in search of orders. After his monthly order getting the pills and potions were made up and distributed by Pennine bus. Similarly, orders were given for fish and chips and the driver would collect them from John Andrew's shop in the Shambles at Settle. They were supplied really hot, well wrapped, and distributed by Pennine on the return journey.

In the days when there was a Hellifield - Gisburn service on auction days Lionel Thornton, the driver, was annoyed by a farmer who requested him to get a move on as he wanted to get the milking done that night. Lionel promptly removed the steering wheel by unscrewing a nut and handing the wheel to the farmer saying "if you can do any better do it".

When Pennine purchased the new AEC *Regal* coach WX 7431 in 1931 it allowed the Company to run private excursions and many loads of dancers were transported to dances in the villages including to Hollins, the wooden village constructed when Stocks Reservoir was being built in the upper Hodder Valley. Not only short excursions were operated but when Harry Fletcher drove a day trip from Barnoldswick to Rhyl it was thought to be daring. Harry drove another party to Gretna Green returning through the Lakes - the passengers had never been so far before. WX 7431 was the subject of a wretched doggerel which went:-

Pennine conductress Nellie Hudson was photographed in front of one of the Company's 1929/30 Leyland buses, either WX 3735 or CK 4295. This picture was taken at Malham before returning on service to Skipton. F.Holmes

A gathering of bus crews at the Three Horse Shoes, Ingleton where coaches stopped for refreshments. Left to right - John Preston, Walter Bates, Ferdie King, John Coates and Fred Holmes. In the background is a 1929/30 Leyland belonging to Pennine Motors and in front of that a 1937-9 maroon and cream Yorkshire Services livery West Yorkshire Road Car Company Leyland Tiger dating from 1929-31. This along with 17 others had been re-bodied in the period 1935-7 with 29 seat Eastern Counties coach bodies and renumbered in the series 552-569. F.Holmes

Posing for their picture were Pennine bus crew - left to right - Frank Ellis, Fred Holmes and D.Mitton. The location was opposite the Old George Hotel, Skipton. F.Holmes

I think that you will agree with me
that its a very tricky bus this AEC.
In case of emergency then great skill is required.
The condition of the steering leaves much to be desired
Perhaps it is the foot brake that causes deflection,
For when you apply it you change direction.
The gears are a curse, I'll tell you what for
You'se swear that the lever was screwed to the floor.
The driver thinks he's performed a wonderful feat.
After wriggling his way up into the seat.
The bus on the whole would look better for painting.
But it's hardly worth while for its disintigrating.

It was not always a well ordered group of passengers and children could be the worst. Harry Addyman was driving school children between Gargrave and Bell Busk one day in the mid-1930s when a fight broke out. He stopped the bus but was attacked by boys hanging round his neck and so he ejected three of them, leaving them by the side of the road at Coniston Cold from where they had to walk home. This attack was actually worse than anything carried out today.

Christmas was a time when the travelling public showed their appreciation for help and services and gifts of chickens, chocolates, cigarettes and similar were made to Pennine staff. Although quite illegal there were invitations to stop the bus and "come inside and have a drink". Some Conductors could not balance their ticket money afterwards! Christmas Day for Pennine used to be the most profitable day of the year allowing those workers who lived on farms or on lodgings to join their families for Christmas dinner and then return to their lodgings all within the day. Before the coming of the bus this had never been possible. All staff received a 10/- bonus for working Christmas Day. Times change and Pennine no longer work on Christmas Day due to lack of passengers.

PASSENGERS (Public Liability).

It is hereby understood and agreed that this Policy extends to cover under section 1 (Public Liability) the Insured's Legal Liability in respect of death or injury to 348. passengers and/or other persons not in the service of the Insured, sustained whilst entering into, riding in, or dismounting from any vehicle described in the schedule herein.

Provided always that the Company's Liability shall not exceed the sum of £ UNLIMITED. (------------------UNLIMITED------------------------) in respect of any one passenger, and in all the sum of £ UNLIMITED. (-------------------- UNLIMITED---------------------------------) in respect of any one accident.
Provided always that in the event of any accident occurring whilst the vehicle is carrying a greater number of passengers than that which it authorised to carry and for which premium has been paid, the Insured shall bear a rateable share of the total loss under this endorsement.

SCHEDULE REFERRED TO HEREIN.

Registered Letter and Number.	Make of Vehicle.	Type of Body.	Year of Make.	Horse Power or Weight of Vehicles including its maximum carrying capacity.	Number of Passengers (if any).	Insured's Estimate of Present Value.	Number of Trailers.*	Warranted Used Only for the Following Purposes.
AS PER SCHEDULE ATTACHED HERETO.								

It is hereby understood and agreed that the Ebor Trading Co. Ltd., of 92, Walmgate, York, are interested in this Insurance under a Hire-Purchase Agreement in respect of vehicles W.W.9531 - W.W.9817 - W.W.9818 - W.X.2979 - W.X.3735 and W.X.3736.

* A trailer is insured by this Policy only whilst actually in use as a trailer to the insured Vehicle and not whilst detached therefrom out of use.

In witness whereof this Policy has been signed for and on behalf of the Company this Fourteenth day of April 1930.

MINED ......

ERED E.B.

.... DIRE

In 1938 Arthur Simpson went on holiday to Germany and on his return advised that there would be a War. So over 300 tyres were purchased and these were stacked in rows 12ft high in the garage, in the stores and upstairs in what had been a hayloft when it was the stables for the Inn in the coaching days. During the entire War no new tyres were purchased, they were retreaded by Ondura at Keighley. 18 machines doing 600,000 miles a year - what colosal forsight!

They also purchased eight Ribble buses which were put into Uncles mill at New Brighton just to scavenge for spares, seats, etc. On a personal note they also bought 1 cwt of sugar each and 7lb tins of Canadian Honey and boxes of tea. Later during the blitz Uncle used the lorry of local haulier Rupert Aldham to go to London to purchase a load of antiques, including Tompion clocks and Beckstein pianos. The Ribble buses purchased for spares were brought to Gargrave and the tanks filled with petrol and the cap locked. When they came to use it someone had already drilled a small hole then after draining the petrol, filled the tank with a wood plug.

Simpson Brothers also had a taxi business but that closed in the War years. The Rolls Royce would start just by turning on the ignition. So perfect was the timing compression and spark.

On 18 August 1939 Pennine employed 34 people but by November the same year this number had dwindled to 16 due to call-up of the rest into the forces. At that time the Company ran 600,000 miles annually with 18 vehicles. The fleet was then reduced by two in September 1939 when AWX 763 and AWX 764 were requisitioned and converted into 8 stretcher ambulances. Painted grey they and Pennine drivers, F.Holmes, and J.Horsman, also requisitioned, were stationed at Bell Isle, Wakefield, home of the West Riding Automobile Co., placed there in readiness for any attack by German bombers. Both drivers were paid a special rate of £3-18-6 per week instead of the normal wage of £2-18-6, the extra pound being for board and lodging. A small payment was made for the hire of these buses. Wages remained static at an average of £2-18-0 per week but the hours worked increased out of all proportion and all remaining staff and the partners kept the services running from 8am to 5pm with just sandwiches for lunch, but home for tea. Then back at 6pm until 8pm to keep the vehicles on the road. Much longer hours were worked if a major accident occured or other problems in which case it might be all-night work. Then of course there were Home Guard duties nightly on Black Park at Eastby. Rifles were kept at home in the corner by the fireplace. In January 1940 there were two Conductresses and by December 1941 this figure had increased to ten. For Christmas 1941 a bonus was paid to Drivers who had left for the forces. This was either £5 or £2-10-0 dependant on length of service. Bonuses had also been paid in 1940 at rates between £3 and £6-10-0 at which time the Drivers wage was £3-7-6. This latter bonus was no doubt compensation for the efforts made during the staff shortages of 1939/40. These bonuses would have been allowed against excess profits. During the War the last three years profits were averaged and anything made over that figure was confiscated by the Government. By June 1940 the number of employees rose to 23 and at the end of the War Pennine employed 47 of which some 11 worked on maintenance due the the deplorable condition of buses which had taken a severe hammering through the War years. About this period the average wage was £5, with 2/- National Insurance, tax varied between 2/- and 7/-.

The big snow of 1947 was a hard time and no less than six buses were stuck in the snow, one at Malham, for a month, one at Airton, one at Long Preston and one at Settle and two half way to Skipton carrying the workers from Johnson & Johnson's. Two police cars got stuck on a hill and were not visible. Other casualties of the weather included one coach belonging to Alec Thompson(Sutton)and one belonging to Wilds (Barnoldswick), also two wagons. Everyone had to walk to Skipton. The radiator water was drained and after some days we were asked to move the buses. Arthur, Vic, Jimmy Crook, Jack Maud, Ernest Collings and Peter Beckwith walked down with a watering can to fill the radiators from the beck. The road was still blocked to Gargrave but the Italian Prisoners of War had dug a single track from Skipton to where the vehicles were stuck. Each bus had to be swung by hand as they were old Petrol *Tigers* . At Malham the Clays drove them down to Gargrave through the fields. At Long Preston Walter Bates started the bus up every hour through the night to stop it freezing. In the morning he walked home to Settle on the railway line. At Ingfield bridge he was rescued and as he was all in had to be helped home. The bus radiators froze up(there was no anti-freeze)in the garage, 40 gallon drums were filled with coke and every now and again pulled outside to riddle and smoke. The coke heap was white-washed to stop thieves. The old Dennis had radiator tubes round the starting handle hole which froze. It had to be drained every night. Percy Shuttleworth made mufflers with prestuds to cover the radiators.

STATEMENT. PENNINE MOTOR SERVICES

Ministry of Health,
Regional Offices, Century House,
South Parade, Leeds 1.

Grouse Garage,
GARGRAVE,
Via Skipton.

To converted omnibuses "Standing By" at Belle Isle, Wakefield.

(a) Standing charge for vehicles.

Index marks and regist'n numbers.	Date of first regist'n	Number of stretchers carried in special fitments provided for the purpose.	Period covered by claim.	Number of days claimed	Daily rate claimed.	Amount claimed.
A.W.X.763.	24.3.36	Eight	1.10.44 to 30.11.44	61	£1.1.0.	£64.1.0.
A.W.X.764.	24.3.36	Eight	1.10.44 to 30.11.44	61	£1.1.0	£64.1.0.

(b) Running charges made for journeys under orders of Hospital Officer.

Date.	Particulars of journeys.	Mileage	Rate per mile.	Amount claimed.
6.10.44	AWX.763. Westgate Station, Wakefield, Pinderfields Hospital.	5.5	3.8d	
	AWX.764. As AWX.763.	5.5	3.8d	£0.3.6d

(c) Drivers Wages. Nil.
(d) Payment. Total amount now claimed to be due .... £128.5.6.
(e) Certificate.
The above claim has been prepared in accordance with the terms and conditions set out in Form A.G.D.44/53/13. The vehicles shown under (a) have been withdrawn from use as public service vehicles and held continuously available for use as ambulance throughout the period stated.

P.P.PENNINE MOTOR SERVICES

J.Windle
Partner.

Dated. 5.1.45.

Two new buses were put into service in 1947 - these were GWT 317/8 a pair of Tiger's with Burlingham bodies. The first of the pair is seen at Skipton. Note the spelling of Malham on the destination screen - this blind remained in use on other buses for several years. The incorrect spelling was attributed to a 'mistake'.

The late R.F.Mack
Tony Edwards collection

GWT 318 at Gargrave, bound for Skipton.

Pennine collection

No new vehicles were available so it was necessary to re-body WX 2979 which got a new utility front entrance bus body in 1944. One of the 1929 *Tigers* WW 9817 received a 30 seat front entrance coach body which was eventually passed on to AWX 764. In 1950 the AEC coach WX 7431 was fitted with a 34 seat front entrance bus body. Parkers Dennis *Lance 1* YG 3405 received a utility front entrance body in 1945. Four ex-Lancashire United Transport buses were purchased from a scrapyard in South Yorkshire and driven home to Gargrave - these were ATE 801/2/3/4. Only the first and the last entered service, the other two being placed in the croft and cannibalised for spares.

The War years were difficult for Pennine Motor Services as indeed they were for all bus companies. No new rolling stock was purchased until 1947 and between this year and late 1951 when purchase of half-cab vehicles came to an end for Pennine, only 9 vehicles were added to the fleet(2 coaches and 7 buses). Due to non-availability from the chassis and body manufacturers, four of these were second-hand.

ADDITIONS TO FLEET 1947-1951
POST-WAR ACQUISITIONS

Registration No.	Make	Chassis No.	Body Made By	Type	New	In to Service	Out of Service	Disposal	Notes
GWT 317	Leyland Tiger	462770	Burlingham	S35F	8/47	8/47*	8/61	A	7
GWT 318	Leyland Tiger	471323	Burlingham	S35F	9/47	9/47*	1/60	A	7
JX 3424	AEC Regal	06621776	C.H.Roe	S32R	/35	3/49	8/55	Scrapped	1
JX 6560	AEC Regal	06622946	Park Royal	S32R	/38	4/49	11/52	Scrapped	2
HYG 60	Leyland Tiger	492039	Wilkes & Meade	C33F	5/39	8/49*	1/62	Scrapped	6,8
HYG 309	Leyland Tiger	493362	Burlingham	C33F	9/49	9/49*	5/65	Scrapped	6,9
JWT 724	Leyland Tiger	496422	Burlingham	S34F	5/50	5/50*	12/63	Scrapped	5,10
ATE 801	Leyland Tiger	9328	Metro Cammel	S32F	/36	10/51	10/56	Scrapped	3,11
ATE 804	Leyland Tiger	9331	Metro Cammel	S32F	/36	11/51	10/56	Scrapped	4,11

* Purchased New S = Service Bus C = Coach F = Front Entrance R = Rear Entrance

Notes:

1. Purchased second-hand from Halifax City Transport. Ex- No.29.
2. Purchased second-hand from Halifax City Transport. Ex- No.57.
3. Purchased second-hand. Ex- Lancashire United No.1.
4. Purchased second-hand. Ex- Lancashire United No.4.
5. Converted for one-man operation. Following withdrawal the engine block was machined by Varley's of Skipton and converted to horizontal for use in a Royal Tiger.
6. Cream and orange coach livery when new. Later orange bus livery used.
7. Leyland PS1.
8. Leyland PS1.1.
9. Leyland PS2.3.
10. Leyland PS2.1.
11. Leyland PS7.

Disposal: A. Sold for school work to an operator in the Runcorn, Chester or Conahs Quay area.

JX 3424 was a 1935 AEC Regal which came to Pennine in 1949 and was formerly Halifax City Transport No.29.
Pennine collection

Two new coaches were added to the fleet in 1949 in the shape of HYG 60 and HYG 309. The former had a Wilkes & Meade 33 seat body and was the first to carry a new coaching livery of cream and orange.When this photograph was taken it had been repainted in bus livery of orange with a black roof and mudguards and either a gray or a cream flash.

The late R.F.Mack
Tony Edwards collection

HYG 309 was the second vehicle to carry the new coaching livery of cream with orange roof, mudguards and flash, but at one time this pair carried bus livery of orange, black and either a gray or a cream flash. It is not known when the bus livery was applied. Pennine collection

HYG 309 carried a Burlingham 33 seat body and when photographed was similarly painted to HYG 60 in bus livery.

Tony Edwards collection

In 1960 the garage staff modified JWT 724, a 1950 Burlingham bodied bus, to air-ram door operation and moved the near side cab window out over the engine, installing a triangular piece of plywood and opening the bulk-head windows behind the driver to permit one-man operation. Frank Ellis became the first one-man operator permanently on the Malham route. No further progress was made on OMO until the Windles left in 1967 but within three years the firm was 100% one-man operation with a consequential reduction in employees from 33 to 23.

The passenger door side of JWT 724. This bus was converted for one-man operation but the conversion is not clearly visible in this photograph.

Pennine collection

Lower: Seen at Settle JWT 724 was obtained new in 1950.

Pennine Collection

After the end of the War new buses were virtually impossible to get and it became necessary for Pennine to extend the life of some of the older vehicles by re-bodying them. Extra vehicles were acquired by purchasing second-hand. Those re-bodied were WW 9817 with coach body, WX 2979, WX 7431 and YG 3405. WW 9817 was a 1929 Leyland Tiger service bus and this acquired a new coach body in the mid-1940s and was painted all-over orange. Driver Fred Holmes stands next to his bus in 1946. F.Holmes

About 1953 AWX 764 received the coach body off WW 9817 when it was withdrawn and is here seen in the orange and cream coach livery at Skipton Bus Station. D.Binns

Pennine purchased four second-hand 1936 Tigers and made two useable vehicles from the four. ATE 804 was ex-Lancashire United and entered service with Pennine in late 1951. It was to serve for another five years. Photographed at Skipton before departure for Settle. D.Binns

ATE 801 without a destination blind, was photographed on Skipton High Street outside the Public Library. Behind, JWT 724 was bound for Lancaster on a wet day.

Pennine collection

Another of the pre-War buses - a Leyland Lion WX 2979 - received a utility bus body in 1944 and was photographed climbing Buckhaw Brow, west of Settle in June 1949. Pennine collection

The 1931 AEC Regal Coach - WX 7431 was fitted out with a new bus body in 1950 and received an AEC diesel engine in the following year. Tony Edwards collection

In the post-war years services operated were:-

Settle Market - Tosside(Temperance Hotel)via Rathmell and Wigglesworth(Tuesdays).
Skipton(bus station) - Malham(Buck Hotel)via Gargrave, Eshton, Newfield and Airton(daily. Joint with Ribble).
Skipton(bus station) - Morecambe(Euston Road bus station)via Gargrave, Coniston Cold, Hellifield, Long Preston Settle, Giggleswick, Austwick, Clapham, Ingleton, Burton-in-Lonsdale, High Bentham, Low Bentham, Millhouses, Wray, Hornby, Brookhouse, Caton and Lancaster(joint with Ribble).
Skipton - Tosside(daily).

Excursions and trips to the seaside, races and similar venues were operated from Skipton, Hellifield, Long Preston and Settle.

Pennine also participated in the Leeds - Morecambe express service of the Yorkshire Pool, but its buses were seldom employed on this service, their mileage share being worked off on stage carriage services between Skipton and Morecambe, this being with the co-operation of Ribble.

As noted earlier in this book Pennine established their headquarters, main garage and offices at Grouse Garage in Gargrave. Here vehicles are routinely maintained, fuelled and overhauled, the staff being able to undertake all jobs. As the years went by, alterations were needed at Grouse Garage - the doorways were too low and an extension was needed in which buses could be painted, also two 30ft pits were wanted. All these needs were undertaken by Pennine themselves and because they did the work the cost was only £70 approx excluding labour. A corrugated shed was erected at Grouse Garage in the 1950s to house the new buses, the older brick garage only able to cope with two vehicles instead of four. The Company's offices open out onto the main street where vehicles were once fuelled.

Pennine had need for a small garage to accomodate two 36ft buses at Settle and it was reported in *Commercial Motor* for 9 August 1963 "that a new garage is to be provided at Settle for buses up to 36ft long". a piece of land was purchased off a Mr Smith who was a garage proprietor in Settle and a good stone garage was built by Mansard(builders)and soon provided a home for the two buses outstationed which had previously had to sleep out. Considerable damage can be done to buses standing out in all weathers not to mention starting problems and cold seats for passengers. The stone for the Royal Oak Garage in Settle came from the old Grammar School building at Giggleswick when it was demolished. The company also had a garage at Ingleton where four vehicles were housed. Whilst this is currently outside Pennine's operating area the garage is used as a vehicle

MTC 757 was the first Royal Tiger to enter service with Pennine in late 1951 at which time it was just over one year old. It had previously been a Leyland demonstrator. When delivered MTC 757 was painted in two shades of blue and had blue upholstery. It was the first Pennine vehicle to have a full front and brought the Company into a new age. Note the ownership 'P.M.S' on the front of the bus. It was scrapped in August 1967 after 16 years service and with 825,000 miles on the clock. The late R.F.Mack R.Platt collection store and as an outstation by Ribble. Mention has been made previously of the original Albion Square garage in Skipton and of the present Skipton depot which became operational in 1956. The Partners and their sons were adaptable and could turn their hands to almost any job including driving and conducting and to a lesser extent building work as exemplified by the construction of the present Skipton garage built in 9 months when 30ft vehicles were introduced.

In November 1951 a new era was born when Pennine Motor Services took delivery of its first full fronted vehicle - a Leyland *Tiger* underfloor engined 44-seat bus purchased from Leyland as an ex-demonstrator and registered MTC 757. This had a hand-made Brush body and its engine carried the number '1'. From this date no more half-cab vehicles were purchased. A second Leyland demonstrator - arrived in September 1952 in the shape of a superb coach registered MTD 235. Both these vehicles had been exhibited at the Commercial Motor Show. This was also a Leyland *Royal Tiger* with an underfloor engine numbered '6'. It had run trials in Ireland where it turned over and bent its chassis.

During the period November 1951 to the end of 1972 twenty-one vehicles were added to the fleet(excluding the vehicles acquired as a result of the Ezra Laycock take-over which are discussed later). One, VTD 214 had a vertical engine, whilst the other twenty were under-floor engined. These were:-

Above: MTD 235 was photographed at Gargrave.
Pennine Collection

Entering Skipton bus station MTD 235 was bound for Bradford on contract, very probably the joint Keswick - Bradford Yorkshire service. Pennine collection

Pennine hold several fleet lists and even though built up in their own offices, there are differences. These occur for dates in and out of service and disposals also vary. The lists in this book are as correct as it is possible to make them.

PURCHASES 1951-1971

Registration No.	Make	Chassis No.	Body Built by	Type	New	In to Service	Out of Service	Disposal	Notes
MTC 757	Leyland Royal Tiger	495666	Brush	S43F	9/50	11/51	8/67	Scrapped	1
MTD 235	Leyland Royal Tiger	502300	Leyland	C41C	10/50	9/52	2/70	A	2
LWY 702	Leyland Royal Tiger	530366	Leyland	S44F	3/53	3/53*	2/70	Scrapped	5
NWT 329	Leyland Royal Tiger	540388	C.H.Roe	S44F	5/54	5/54*	1/74	B	6
NWT 807	Leyland Royal Tiger	540158	C.H.Roe	DP44F	6/54	6/54*	6/74	Scrapped	6
VDT 214	Leyland Comet	543095	Duple	C36F	/55	12/55	8/61	C	1
UWX 277	Leyland Tiger Cub	577131	Duple Mid	DP41F	5/58	5/58*	6/73	D	7
6108 WU	Leyland Tiger Cub	596827	Duple Mid	DP41F	4/60	4/60*	4/73	E	7
9712 WX	Leyland Tiger Cub	607602	Duple Mid	DP41F	5/61	5/61*	6/72	E	7
5895 YG	Leyland Leopard	612555	Duple Mid	DP41F	1/62	1/62*	5/74	F	8
240 CWY	Leyland Leopard	629206	C.H.Roe	S41F	5/63	5/63*	8/75	E	8
ECK 610	Leyland Royal Tiger	520914	Leyland	S44F	/52	1/64	6/77	Scrapped M	3,5
FWX 554C	Leyland Leopard	L40609	Plaxton	C49F	5/65	5/65*	8/71	J	9,10
LWU 499D	Leyland Leopard	61086	C.H.Roe	S49F	6/66	6/66*	7/78	E	11
UWU 521F	Leyland Leopard	800408	Willowbrook	DP41F	4/68	4/68*	by 7/70	L	11
CWT 474H	Leyland Leopard	901376	Willowbrook	DP49F	12/69	12/69*	9/84	G	12
CWU 101H	Leyland Leopard	903917	Willowbrook	DP49F	2/70	2/70*	by 7/84	N	12
HWU 816J	Leyland Leopard	7104591	Willowbrook	DP49F	3/71	3/71*	by 7/84	N	12
HWU 817J	Leyland Leopard	7101138	Willowbrook	DP49F	8/71	8/71*	5/87	N	13
OWR 265K	Leyland Leopard	7200755	Plaxton Elite	C49F	4/72	4/72*	4/91	H	13
OWR 266K	Leyland Leopard	7200756	Plaxton Elite	C49F	6/72	6/72*	4/91	H	13

* Purchased New   S = Service Bus   C = Coach   DP = Dual Purpose Vehicle
F = Front Entrance   C = Centre Entrance(MTD 235)

Notes:

1. Ex- Leyland demonstrator. PSU1.13.
2. Ex- Leyland demonstrator. First seen at Commercial Vehicle Show. PSU1.15.
3. Purchased second-hand from Ribble Motor Services. Out of service 6/71 or 6/77.
5. PSU1.17.
6. PSU1.14.
7. PSUC1.2.
8. L2.
9. PSU3.3R.
10. Cream and orange coach livery when new.
11. PSU4.3R.
12. PSU3.A.4R.
13. PSU3.B.4R.

Disposal:

A. Currently(1999)stored in Baroldswick garage of Pennine. Hoped eventually to restore.
B. Sold to Port of Liverpool Authority for further service. Over 1,000,000 miles when sold.

C. Sold to Bronte, Haworth for further service. Then sold for preservation.
D. Sold to Brown's, Guildford, Surrey, 6/1973.
E. Sold to Tillingbourne Valley, Guildford, Surrey, for further service.
F. Sold to Beresford, Leek for further service 5/1974.
G. Sold to Border, Barnoldswick for further service.
H. Scrapped at Gargrave for spares early 1991.
J. Sold to Jones, Pwllheli 10/1971(via Yates).
L. Sold to Tetley, Leeds 7/1970. Sold prematurely because of small number of seats.
M.Used for spares.
N.Withdrawn 1983/4. Still in field at Gargrave 1986.

A later view of LWY 702 which has now acquired a front end grill.

Pennine collection

UXW 277 was a Leyland Tiger Cub with a 41 seat Duple body, which was new in 1958. It was seen en-route for Lancaster in its first year of service.

Pennine collection

MTD 235 was a Leyland Royal Tiger demonstrator which had been seen originally at the Commercial Vehicle Show and which came into the Pennine fleet in September 1952 when nearly two years old. It was photographed in Skipton Bus Station in 1957. Pennine collection.

LWY 702 was photographed on service to Ingleton with ATE 801 following on a Settle service. This latter was one of the two buses made out of four second-hand ones after the War. Pennine collection

Passenger door side of NWT 807. This photograph shows the clean lines of this pair of Roe -bodied buses.
Pennine collection

Looking towards the back of the bus showing the attractive upholstery used on NWT 329 and 807. Pennine collection

In 1954 a pair of Leyland Royal Tiger buses with Roe bodywork were purchased new. These were registered NWT 329 and NWT 807. Our photograph shows the drivers side of NWT 807.

Pennine collection

An official photograph showing the interior of one of the pair of Royal Tiger's registered NWT 329 and NWT 807. View looking forward to front of bus.

Pennine collection

UWX 277 was a Leyland Tiger Cub with a 41 seat Duple body which was new in 1958. The two photographs show both sides.
Pennine collection

Opposite Page: Two interior views of UWX 277, Top: looking towards the front of the bus, and Lower: looking towards the rear. On this vehicle the door was hand-operated.
Pennine collection(both)

VTD 214 was a 1955 Leyland Comet demonstrator which Pennine acquired and ran until 1961 when it was sold to Bronte, Haworth, due to its small seating capacity of 36. Note 'PMS' in the circle on the body side - the only time ownership was thus depicted.
Pennine collection

A front view of VDT 214.
Pennine collection

En- route to Ingleton 240CWY passes the Pennine H.Q. in Gargrave.

The late R.F.Mack Tony Edwards collection

An experimental layout was tried on this 1966 Leopard in an effort to gain extra seating. From front to back the normal 2+2 was used, then 4 sets of seats 2+3 and a rear seat for 6. Officially, LWU 499D was a 49 seater. Pennine collection

A second Tiger Cub was purchased new in 1960 and registered 6108 WU. The new bus was a 41 seat dual purpose vehicle and this photograph shows quite well its handsome lines.

Pennine collection

5895 YG was a similar vehicle but was a Leopard new in 1962. Here seen on contract passing the Bus Station at Skipton.

The late R.F.Mack
Pennine collection

A similar vehicle - 9712 WX - was added to the fleet in 1961 and is here seen in Poulton Road Coach Park in Morecambe on a contract job.

Pennine collection

LWU 499D was photographed in July 1957 outside Gargrave railway station.
Pennine collection

A second view of the experimental seating arrangements used on LWU 499D - this time looking towards the front of the bus.
Pennine collection

A 41 seat Willowbrook dual purpose vehicle - UWU 521F - entered the fleet in 1968 but had been sold on by July 1970, probably due to its low seating capacity.

Pennine collection

Below: CWU 101H was one of four similar Leopards with 49 seat Willowbrook bodies new between 1969 and 1971. Location Skipton Bus Station. J.Winkley

HWU 816J and 817J were Willowbrook bodied 49 seat dual purpose vehicles, entering the fleet in 1971. The latter was photographed in Skipton Bus Station.

J.Winkley

ECK 610 was purchased second-hand from Ribble Motor Services. New in 1952 it entered service for Pennine in 1964 and was out of service by mid-1977. Both pictures are taken at Skipton Bus Station. The lower picture is interesting as the vehicle has had its front end patched with a piece from another bus!
Tony Edwards and Pennine collections

Another coach was added to the fleet when FWX 554C was purchased new in 1965. This 'Leopard' did not last long and was out of service 6 years later being sold to Jones, Pwllheli in October of that year. D.Binns collection

5 THE EZRA LAYCOCK ACQUISITION AND THE 1970s

As the years passed each partners son came into the business so that there were six families in the Pennine partnership. Jim and Alan Windle sold out in 1967. There was however much bitterness with the property being re-valued for Council Tax and there was bitterness in other ways which led to Arthur Simpson drawing up a new partnership agreement to stop anyone making a killing in the future.

1972 was a milestone in Pennine history for in that year the business and vehicles of Ezra Laycock Ltd, Barnoldswick, was acquired. Laycock had earlier acquired the Silver Star business owned by J.T.Hey with a service from Carleton to Skipton.

An alteration was soon made to the Skipton - Carleton and Skipton - Barnoldswick route by combining the two, the route becoming Skipton - Carleton, then proceeding down Heslaker Lane at the end of which the main road was rejoined for the rest of the original route to Barnoldswick.

Pennine thus acquired the business of the company described as the operators of "the first bus in Yorkshire" becoming the only independent survivor in this area. The exact date and time of the transfer was midnight on 11 August 1972.

The following Laycock vehicles were involved in the sale to Pennine:

SINGLE-DECKERS: EX- EZRA LAYCOCK AUGUST 1972

Registration No.	Make	Chassis No.	Body Built by	Type	New	Into Service	Out of Service	E.Laycock Fleet No.	Notes
OWX 144	Bristol LS5G		ECW	C41F	/55			84	B2, M
XHW 401	Bristol LS5G	117105	ECW	S45F	/59	8/72	1/73	89	A, S,Z
XHW 408	Bristol LS5G	117128	ECW	S45F	/59	8/72	1/73	85	A1, T,Z
XHW 409	Bristol LS5G	117129	ECW	S45F	/59	8/72	4/73	86	A1, U,Z
RWW 977	Bristol LS5G	117036	ECW	S45F	/59	8/72	1/73	94	B, W,Z
RWW 985	Bristol LS5G	117053	ECW	S45F	/59	8/72	1/73	95	B1, W,Z
MYG 759K	Bedford YRQ	298319	Plaxton	C45F	5/72	8/72	4/75	90	R,Y
MYG 760K	Bedford YRQ	298323	Plaxton	C45F	5/72	8/72	5/75	91	P,Y
MYG 761K	Bedford YRQ	2298318	Plaxton	C53F	7/72	8/72	5/75	92	R,Y
OWY 197K	Leyland Leopard	7200891	Plaxton	C53F	7/72	8/72	after /92	93	N,X,Y,Z

Notes:

A. Purchased by Ezra Laycock from Bristol Omnibus Company 9/1971.
A1.Purchased by Ezra Laycock from Bristol Omnibus Company 11/1970.
B. Purchased by Ezra Laycock from West Yorkshire Road Car Company 12/1971.
B1.Purchased by Ezra Laycock from West Yorkshire Road Car Company 11/1971.
B2.Purchased by Ezra Laycock from West Yorkshire Road Car Company 4/1970.
M. Purchased by Ezra Laycock from West Yorkshire Road Car Company.
N. Stored at Pennine's Ingleton garage for possible future restoration/preservation.
P. Sold to Taylor, Penrith, 3.1975.
R. Sold to Priory, North Shields, 3.1975.
S. Sold to Winn, Whiston.
T. Sold to APC. Dungeness.
U. Sold to Allander, Milngavie.
W. Sold to Silcox, Pembroke Dock.
X. Leyland PSU3.B.4R.
Y. Re-painted in Pennine livery.
Z. Some of the Bristols were operated for a short time after aquisition, mostly on the Skipton - Carleton run. Non were painted in Pennine livery.

DOUBLE-DECKERS

Registration No.	Make	New	In to Service	Out of Service	EL No.	Notes
BCK 437	Leyland Titan PD1A	/47	-	6/72	74	1
BCK 428	Leyland Titan PD1A	/47	-	10/69	75	1,4
BCK 452	Leyland Titan PD1A	/47	-	5/72	76	1,4
ECK 927	Leyland Titan PD2/12	/52	-	/52	80	2
968 CWL	AEC Regent V	/58	-	7/72	83	3

Notes:

1. Purchased by Ezra Laycock from Ribble Motor Services 7/1966. 53 seats. Not run by Pennine.
2. Purchased by Ezra Laycock from Ribble Motor Services 8/1968. 53 seats. Not run by Pennine, sold for scrap.
3. Purchased by Ezra Laycock from City of Oxford Motor Services 1/1970. 65 seats. Not run by Pennine. Sold to Wild Bros, Barnoldswick.
4. These are not shown on Pennine lists. The others are thought not to have been operated by Pennine.

Thus it will be seen that only the four new coaches(Ezra Laycock Fleet No's 90-93)were repainted by Pennine in the familiar orange, black and grey livery. As a reminder as to origin, "Pennine" was rendered in green and white. The three Bedfords were sold in 1975 but Leyland *Leopard* OWY 179K was almost exactly to Pennine's own specification, and was thus incorporated within the fleet. This vehicle still exist in 1999 and it is hoped to eventually restore it for special duties. OWY 179K is currently in store at the Ingleton garage. One or more of the Bristol/ECW single-deck buses was operated on the Carleton route for a week by Pennine. Part of the Barnoldswick premises were given away to Laycock's partner to complete the deal, and the

OWY 197K was one of the vehicles taken over in the Ezra Laycock acquisition and one of only four Laycock buses to be repainted in Pennine colours. T.Edwards

remainder became home for the two service buses used on the route to Skipton. Barnoldswick is(1999)also the home for MTD 235 the Motor Show coach which hopefully might re-emerge one day fully restored.

There was a reduction in Laycock staff from 16 to 5 and a vehicle reduction from 14 to 4. The routes added were Skipton via Carleton to Barnoldswick. Also acquired was Wilds service from Barnoldswick to Gargrave for Johnson & Johnson's. Before the sale Laycock worked a number of school contracts and in order to work these he purchased many older buses both single and double-decker. Amongst these contracts was one from Barnoldswick to Skipton baths charged at 10/- per trip. Pennine did not want these non-lucrative contracts and gave the school contracts away. Despite this generosity one fool undercut everybody else through greed. Six additional buses were added to the fleet between 1973 and 1975:

ADDED TO FLEET 1973-1975

Registration No.	Make	Chassis No.	Body Built by	Type	New	In to Service	Out of Service	Notes
UWX 596L	Leyland Leopard	7300042	Plaxton✱	C49F	2/73	3/73*	A	1,3,4
RWY 378M	Leyland Leopard	7401312	Plaxton✱	C49F	4/74	4/74*	10/80	2,4
RWY 379M	Leyland Leopard	7401481	Plaxton✱	C49F	4/74	4/74*	A	1,4
JWU 797N	Leyland Leopard	7500937	Plaxton✱	C49F	4/75	4/75*	A	1,5
JWU 798N	Leyland Leopard	7500938	Plaxton✱	C49F	6/75	6/75*	A	1,5
JWU 799N	Leyland Leopard	7501076	Plaxton✱	C49F	6/75	6/75*	A	1,5

* Purchased New F = Front Entrance

✱ Elite Express III

Notes:

1. In service 31/4/92.
2. Burnt out 1980.
3. May have been C51F. New 3/1973.
4. Leyland PSU3.B.4R.
5. Leyland PSU3.C.4R.

A. Date unknown.

Ex-Ezra Laycock 1972 Leopard and the wording on the rear showing new ownership insignia. As a reminder to previous ownership 'Pennine' was rendered in green and white. T.Edwards

Six new vehicles - all of the Leyland Leopard/Plaxton combination were purchased new in 1973/4 and 1975 and one of these was subsequently burnt out at Gargrave. This picture of JWU 798N is typical of these 49 seaters.
P.Lason

PENNINE FLEET IN BI-CENTENARY YEAR 1975

Registration No.	New	Make	Chassis No.	Body Made By	Type
CWT 474H	1969	Leyland Leopard PSU3A/4R	901376	Willowbrook	DP49F
CWU 101H	1970	Leyland Leopard PSU3A/4R	903907	Willowbrook	DP49F
HWU 816J	1971	Leyland Leopard PSU3A/4R	70.04591	Willowbrook	DP49F
HWU 817J	1971	Leyland Leopard PSU3B/4R	71.01138	Willowbrook	DP49F
OWR 265K	1972	Leyland Leopard PSU3B/4R	72.00755	Plaxton Elite Express III	C49F
OWR 266K	1972	Leyland Leopard PSU3B/4R	72.00756	Plaxton Elite Express III	C49F
MYG 759K	1972	Bedford YRQ2D2TDOM	298319	Plaxton Elite Express III	C45F
MYG 760K	1972	Bedford YRQ2D2TDOM	298323	Plaxton Elite Express III	C45F
MYG 761K	1972	Bedford YRQ2D2TDOM	298318	Plaxton Elite Express III	C45F
OWY 197K	1972	Leyland Leopard PSU3B/4R	72.00891	Plaxton Elite Express III	C49F
UWX 596L	1973	Leyland Leopard PSU3B/4R	73.00042	Plaxton Elite Express III	C49F
RWY 378M	1974	Leyland Leopard PSU3B/4R	74.01312	Plaxton Elite Express III	C49F
RWY 379M	1974	Leyland Leopard PSU3B/4R	74.01481	Plaxton Elite Express III	C49F
JWU 797N	1975	Leyland Leopard PSU3C/4R	75.00937	Plaxton Elite Express III	C49F
JWU 798N	1975	Leyland Leopard PSU3C/4R	75.00938	Plaxton Elite Express III	C49F
JWU 799N	1975	Leyland Leopard PSU3C/4R	75.01076	Plaxton Elite Express III	C49F

C = Coach DP = Dual Purpose Vehicle F = Front Entrance

Pennine

TOWARDS THE END OF THE CENTURY 6

Circa 1976 Pennine made an application for a tours and excursion licence but after strong opposition from operators like Wallace Arnold, was refused except for tours to Holland which ran for a few years.

The 1980s was a period of declining traffic, mini-bus competition, escalating costs and wages familiar to all bus operators, requiring in the case of Pennine, trimming of services, staff reductions and one-man operation. The Privatisation of Public Transport Act did little to encourage investment and takings no longer justified the high capital outlay of purchasing new buses. Accordingly, with the exception of two new Leyland *Swifts* , all vehicles purchased since 1984 have been second-hand.

FLEET PURCHASES 1975 TO THE END OF THE PLAXTON ERA

Registration No.	Make By.	Chassis	Body Made	Type	New	In to Service	Out of Service
UWR 712R	Leyland Leopard	7607703	Plaxton	C49F	5/77	5/77*	after 4/92
AUA 965S	Leyland Leopard	7705587	Plaxton	C49F	4/78	4/78*	after 4/92
NWT 839V	Leyland Leopard	7904932	Plaxton	C49F	7/80	7/80*	after 4/92
BTL 485X	Leyland Leopard	7930058	Plaxton	C53F	9/81	11/83	
TPL 762X	Leyland Tiger	8101065	Plaxton	C53F	1/82	12/84	10/86
RHE 30M	Leyland Leopard	7305272	Plaxton	C49F	5/74	10/86	4/89
RHE 31M	Leyland Leopard	7400018	Plaxton	C49F	5/74	10/86	by 6/91
RHE 32M	Leyland Leopard	7400019	Plaxton	C49F	5/74	10/86	by 10/89
NPA 220W	Leyland Leopard	8130257	Plaxton	C49F	5/81	10/86	after 4/92
YGE 635S	Leyland Leopard	7701477	Plaxton	C51F	4/78	11/86	after 4/92
SOA 681S	Leyland Leopard	7703876	Plaxton	C49F	4/78	10/86	after 4/92
UDW 140S	Leyland Leopard	7705332	Plaxton	C49F	4/78	1/88	after 4/92
OCK 452T	Leyland Leopard	7802074	Plaxton	C49F	3/79	4/89	after 4/92
OUF 50W	Leyland Leopard	8031147 or 8021147	Plaxton	C49F	4/81	9/90	

UWR 712R Type PSU3.E.4R, bought new, re-registered JIL 7417. Scrapped.

AUA 965S Type PSU3.E.4R, bought new, re-registered JIL 7416. Scrapped.

NWT 839V Type PSU3.E.4R, bought new, re-registered JIL 4698. Fleet No.12. Sold to Northumbrian County Council School Buses. The last Leopard purchased new as a replacement for RWY 378M burnt out in 1980.

BTL 485X Type PSU3.E.4R, acquired from Marfleet, Binbrook, Lincs, then Wings, Sleaford. Re-registered JIL 2426. Does not carry a Fleet number. Orange and cream coach livery. In service late 1999.

TPL 762X Type TR.CIL.11.3R, acquired from Tillingbourne, Gomshall, Surrey. Sold to Gath, Dewsbury(?).

RHE 30M Acquired from Yorkshire Traction, Barnsley, No.30. Never run. To Birmingham 8/89 then Brandish, Nuneaton by 3/92.

RHE 31M Ex-Yorkshire Traction No.31, used for spares by 9/91.

RHE 32M Ex-Yorkshire Traction No.32, used for spares by 9/91.

NPA 220W Acquired from London Country, Riegate. No.P420, re-registered JIL 2428, Fleet No.14. To B&J Travel, Barnoldswick.

YGE 635S Type PSU3.E.4R, new to Garelochhead Coach Services, then Cotterell, Mitcheldean, Glos. To B&J Travel, Barnoldswick.

SOA 681S Ex-Midland Red North, Scrapped.

UDW 140S Ex-Southend Transport, No.354, Scrapped.

OCK 452T	Acquired from Fishwick, Leyland, re-registered JIL 4653 then HWR 449T, converted to wrecker/tow truck at Gargrave and re-registered HWR 449T.
OUF 50W	Ex-Southdown, Brighton, No.1347, re-registered JIL 2427. Still in service late 1999.

According to one of the Pennine lists there was another vehicle, a double-decker but why or indeed if this was purchased is unknown. BKC 288K, Leyland Atlantean, chassis 7200259?, Alexander S75F, New 8/72. Thought to have been ex-Merseyside PTE. Into service with Pennine 9/87, out of service by 8/89. The 'into' and 'out of service' dates are from Pennine lists and are from their own records so this bus, just might have been purchased for a specific job - maybe Johnson & Johnson's works service. No-one remembers this bus but of course it might not have been painted in Pennine colours. There is considerable doubt I feel.

AUA 965S was purchased new in 1978 and this Leopard was photographed reversing into Skipton garage which opened in 1956. P.Lason

'Travel the Pennine Way' was applied to the rear of some Plaxton's and AUA 965S had the added distinction of carrying GB plates - presumably having been used on tours to Holland. Tony Edwards

Bus de-regulation in October 1986 was to prove a mile-stone year for the bus industry to the extent of being the beginning of the end for the rural bus. Immediately prior to this event Pennine was operating three principal routes, that from Skipton to Settle, Skipton to Malham and the ex-Laycock route between Skipton and Barnoldswick. Discussions were held with Ribble as to what was to become of their joint service to Lancaster and Morecambe since a joint working would not be allowed under de-regulation. The route between Skipton and Lancaster could not sustain two operators working seperately. The decision arrived at was that Ribble would operate from Lancaster to Ingleton and Pennine would operate from Ingleton to Skipton. There would be no further through running and in addition Ribble agreed to terminate its X43 Manchester-Skipton service at Nelson so allowing Pennine to operate between Nelson and Skipton. These arrangements were mutually agreed and Pennine met with Ribble management at a hotel near Clitheroe where after dining, Norman Simpson was presented with a framed photograph of an early Pennine TS1 *Tiger*, complete with an engraved plate to mark the end of the joint relationship.

Pennine registered their changes as required by the new legislation proposing a regular hourly service between Skipton and Settle only, with but four journeys daily extended to Ingleton. An extension of their hourly service to Barnoldswick on through erstwhile Ribble territory to Earby and Colne was planned. Like-wise between Skipton and Embsay, a former route of Ribble, and later of the West Yorkshire Road Car Company. A reduced service to Malham was put forth with termination of the Sunday service(the buses up Malhamdale often ran empty, particularly at winter week-ends, the motor car having taken its toll on rural public transport). The Yorkshire Dales are no exception to the car ownership problem with locals and visitors alike causing local bus services to become non-viable, resulting in their withdrawal.

Things however did not work out as planned, the first problem being caused by the North Yorkshire County Council who put the Lancaster-Ingleton service as far as Settle out to tender. Ribble secured this on weekdays with Lancaster City Transport filling in on Sundays. The Pennine timetable was therefor duplicated between Ingleton and Settle with connections at Ingleton becoming difficult.

Problems arose on the Nelson service. The original idea had been to extend the Skipton-Barnoldswick runs to Nelson and not to operate the service as a seperate one via Earby. The Lancashire County Council objected to the Barnoldswick detour, insisting on, two seperate routes, i.e., Skipton-Barnoldswick and Skipton-Nelson via Earby. Pennine agreed to this but when the Lancashire County Council requested them to run on to Burnley, refused because of its arrangement with Ribble to join up with the X43 at Nelson.

The outcome was that the Lancashire County Council put the whole service Skipton-Burnley out to tender. This was secured by Burnley & Pendle. Pennine were not pleased and commenced working from Nelson to Burnley using the Burnley & Pendle main route. This state of affairs continued for some 12 months when Burnley & Pendle found the section between Colne and Skipton to be unprofitable, and withdrew.

Yet another problem was one which affected both Pennine and Burnley & Pendle. A Colne based coach operator, Tyrer's started working over both concern's routes to Burnley from Barnoldswick and Colne. This was resolved by Pennine and Burnley & Pendle buying Tyrer out on a 50/50 basis. No vehicles were involved in the purchase.

New ground and an hourly service came with the registration of a route between Skipton and Eastby via Embsay, once operated by Ribble and by the West Yorkshire Road Car Company since 1976.

A tendered School service from Bolton Abbey was instructed to divert via Embsay and Eastby and as they were paid to do so, charge a lower fare. Pennine then abandoned the Eastby service, but the County Council then withdrew the tendered one. Accordingly Pennine re-started its Eastby morning and afternoon runs to cater for the schoolchildren, and the village now has a bus service on school days only.

A further change was the take-over of Skipton local services worked for many years previously by the West Yorkshire Road Car Company. These involved the Horse-Close and Greatwood Estates, a circular service later to take in a newer housing estate - Moorview - arrived at by a detour off Shortbank Road.

An extra problem was caused by three ex-Pennine drivers setting up a new company - Skipton Busways, competing with Pennine on the Skipton local services and also over some routes of Keighley & District(successor to West Yorkshire). This problem was overcome when Keighley & District bought Skipton Busways out and Pennine then bought Keighley & District local Skipton services.

PENNINE

Serving the Yorkshire Dales

BTL 485X had been purchased in 1983 when only two years old and this photograph shows its first Pennine coaching livery. Reference to the next picture will show that this was slightly simplified in later years. This coach still exists(1999) but is re-registered JIL 2426. Pennine collection

The slightly simplified livery of BTL 485X which was also used on Pennine's tours to Holland.
Tony Edwards

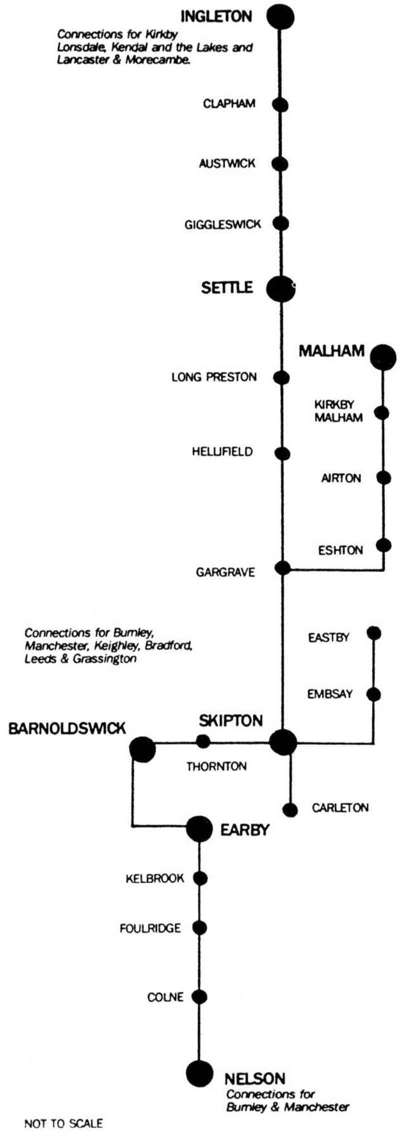

NPA 220W had been new in 1981 but was purchased by Pennine when five years old. Seen on Broughton Road, Skipton en-route to the Bus Station it survived long enough to be re-registered JIL 2428 and to carry fleet No.14. This photograph is interesting since it shows Dewhurst's mill chimney in the course of demolition - each brick was dropped down the centre of the chimney. H.Meyer

FROM 26 OCTOBER 1986

580	SKIPTON · SETTLE · INGLETON
210	SKIPTON · MALHAM
211	SKIPTON · BARNOLDSWICK
212	SKIPTON · CARLETON
214	SKIPTON · EMBSAY · EASTBY
215	SKIPTON · NELSON
216	SKIPTON · HORSE CLOSE CIRCULAR
218	GARGRAVE · BWK/EARBY CIRCULAR

TRAVEL THE PENNINE WAY
BUY PENNINE RETURN TICKETS
THEY ARE CHEAPER IN THE LONG RUN

Pennine Service
580

Skipton · Settle · Ingleton

Monday to Saturday

Code	♦NS	♦S	♦G	♦G		G		F	G		S	NS	G	♦NFS		G	G		♦
Skipton, Bus Station	0635	0735	0735	0845	0945	1045	1145		1245	1345	1445	1445	1545		1645	1745	1845	1945	2220
Gargrave, The Square	0653	0753	0753	0856	0956	1056	1156	1235	1256	1356	1456	1456	1556	1635	1656	1756	1856	1956	2231
Hellifield, Bay Horse	0706	0806	0806	0909	1009	1109	1209	1243	1309	1409	1509	1509	1609	1648	1709	1809	1909	2009	2244
Long Preston, Maypole	0712	0812	0812	0915	1015	1115	1215	1254	1315	1415	1515	1515	1615	1654	1715	1815	1915	2015	2250
Settle, Market Place	0723	0823	0823	0925	1025	1125	1225	1303	1325	1425	1525	1525	1625	1705	1725	1825	1925	2025	2301
Giggleswick, Harts Head	0725	0825	0825	0927	1027	1127			1327	1427		1527	1627		1727	1827	1927	2027	
Four Lane Ends			0830	0930		1130			1330							1830	1930		
Austwick Village Green	0738	0838			1040		1240					1540			1740				
Clapham, Post Office	0743	0843			1045		1245					1545			1745				
Ingleton, 3 Horse Shoes	0754	0854			1056		1256					1556			1756				

Sunday

Skipton, Bus Station	0945	1245	1445	1645	1945
Gargrave, The Square	0956	1256	1456	1656	1956
Hellifield, Bay Horse	1009	1309	1509	1709	2009
Long Preston, Maypole	1015	1315	1515	1715	2015
Settle, Market Place	1025	1325	1525	1725	2025
Giggleswick, Harts Head	1027			1727	
Four Lane Ends					
Austwick Village Green	1040			1740	
Clapham, Post Office	1045			1745	
Ingleton, 3 Horse Shoes	1056			1756	

Pennine Service
580

Ingleton · Settle · Skipton

Monday to Saturday

Code	♦NS		♦NS		GH	S♦				♦F			□	NS	MTh♦				♦
Ingleton, 3 Horse Shoes			0800			0900		1100			1300			1600			1800		
Clapham, Post Office			0811			0911		1111			1311			1611			1811		
Austwick Village Green			0816			0916		1116			1316			1616			1816		
Giggleswick, Harts Head		0735	0829	0827	0927	0929		1129	1227		1329			1629			1829		
Four Lane Ends		0738		0830	0930				1230					S					
Settle, Market Place	0644	0744	0835	0835	0935	0935	1035	1135	1235	1305	1335	1435	1535	1635	1705	1735	1835	1934	2135
Long Preston, Maypole	0654	0754	0845	0845	0945	0945	1045	1145	1245	1315	1345	1445	1545	1645	1715	1745	1815	1945	2145
Hellifield, Bay Horse	0700	0800	0851	0851	0951	0951	1051	1151	1251	1321	1351	1451	1551	1651	1721	1751	1851	1951	2151
Gargrave, The Square	0713	0813	0904	0904	1004	1004	1104	1204	1304	1334	1404	1504	1604	1704	1734	1804	1904	2004	2204
Johnson & Johnson	0715	0815																	
Skipton, Bus Station	0725	0825	0915	0915	1015	1015	1115	1215	1315	1345	1415	1515	1615	1715	1745	1815	1915	2015	2215

Sunday

Ingleton, 3 Horse Shoes		1100				1800
Clapham, Post Office		1111				1811
Austwick Village Green		1116				1816
Giggleswick, Harts Head		1129				1829
Four Lane Ends						
Settle, Market Place	1035	1135	1235	1335	1535	1835
Long Preston, Maypole	1045		1245	1345	1545	1845
Hellifield, Bay Horse	1051		1251	1351	1551	1851
Gargrave, The Square	1104		1304	1404	1604	1904
Johnson & Johnson						
Skipton, Bus Station	1115		1315	1415	1615	1915

Code: ♦ — Works service — liable to suspension if not so required. — Schools service. **F** — Friday only. **NS** — Not Saturday.
NFS — Not Friday or Saturday. **MTh** — Monday to Thursday only. **G** — Giggleswick Circular.
□ — Departs from Settle Bridge. **GH** — Giggleswick Circular Not Saturday. **S** — Saturday only.

Pennine Service
210

Skipton · Malham via Gargrave, Eshton, Airton

Monday to Saturday

Code		♦ NS	WS			Sunday †
Skipton, Waller Hill Bus Station	dep.	0700	0935	1235	1600	1835
Johnson and Johnson Works		0711				
Gargrave, The Square		0713	0946	1246	1611	1846
Eshton, Post Box		0719	0952	1252	1617	1852
Newfield, Guest House		0726	0959	1259	1624	1859
Airton, Chapel		0730	1003	1303	1628	1903
Kirkby Malham, Victoria Hotel		0735	1008	1308	1633	1908
Malham, Buck Hotel	arr.	0740	1013	1313	1638	1913

Monday to Saturday

Code		♦NS	WS			Sunday
Malham, Buck Hotel	dep.	0743	1015	1315	1643	1915
Kirkby Malham, Victoria Hotel		0748	1020	1320	1648	1920
Airton, Chapel		0753	1025	1325	1653	1925
Newfield, Guest House		0757	1029	1329	1657	1929
Eshton, Post Box		0804	1036	1336	1704	1936
Gargrave, The Square		0810	1042	1342	1710	1942
Skipton, Waller Hill Bus Station	arr.	0821	1053	1353	1721	1953

GOOD FRIDAY — NORMAL SERVICE.
BANK HOLIDAY MONDAYS — MAINLY A SATURDAY SERVICE WILL OPERATE — PLEASE CHECK BEFORE TRAVELLING.
FOR TRAFFIC ARRANGEMENTS DURING CHRISTMAS AND NEW YEAR HOLIDAY PERIODS, SEE SEPARATE ANNOUNCEMENTS.
XMAS DAY, BOXING DAY AND NEW YEARS DAY — NO SERVICE.

Code: ♦ — Works service — liable to suspension if not so required. **WS** — Wednesday and Saturday only. **NS** — Not Saturday.
† Summer Only.
Easter Sunday then first Sunday in May to last Sunday in September.

INFORMATION
☎ GARGRAVE 215

PENNINE MOTORS — GROUSE GARAGE, GARGRAVE, NORTH YORKSHIRE

Pennine Service
211

Skipton · Thornton · Barnoldswick

Monday to Saturday															Sunday					
Code	◆	◆C				C					C			*◆						
Skipton, Bus Station	0730	0935	1035	1135	1235	1335	1435	1535	1635	1735	1835	1935	2135	2235	1235	1335	1535	1735	1835	1935
Thornton	0745	0950	1050	1150	1250	1350	1450	1550	1650	1750	1850	1950	2150	2250	1250	1350	1550	1750	1850	1950
Earby, Bus Station	0748													2253						1953
Barnoldswick	0757	1000	1100	1200	1300	1400	1500	1600	1700	1800	1900	2000	2200	2302	1300	1400	1600	1800	1900	2000
Barnoldswick, Farmers Arms		1002	1102	1202	1302	1402	1502	1602	1702	1802	1902	2002	2202	2304						

Pennine Service
211

Barnoldswick · Thornton · Skipton

Monday to Saturday															Sunday				
Code	◆	*◆	C					C						◆					
Barnoldswick		0805	1000	1100	1200	1300	1400	1500	1600	1700	1800	1900	2100	2200	1300	1500	1700	1800	1900
Barnoldswick, Farmers Arms	0635	0807	1002	1102	1202	1302	1402	1502	1602	1702	1802	1902	2102	2202	1302	1502	1702	1802	1902
Barnoldswick	0644	0809	1005	1105	1205	1305	1405	1505	1605	1705	1805	1905	2105	2205	1305	1505	1705	1805	1905
Earby, Bus Station	0649																		
Thornton	0652	0814	1014	1114	1214	1314	1414	1514	1614	1714	1814	1914	2114	2214	1314	1514	1714	1814	1914
Skipton, Bus Station	0707	0840	1030	1130	1230	1330	1430	1530	1630	1730	1830	1930	2130	2230	1330	1530	1730	1830	1930

Code: * — Operates via Carleton. ◆ — Works service — liable to suspension if not so required. C — Operates via Coates Estate.
CHRISTMAS DAY, BOXING DAY AND NEW YEARS DAY — NO SERVICE.

PENNINE WEEKLY TICKETS

FOR REGULAR TRAVELLERS INTO TOWN, WHY NOT BUY A WEEKLY TICKET.
PURCHASED ON A MONDAY MORNING AT NINE TIMES THE SINGLE FARE GIVES FRIDAY AFTERNOON, SATURDAY AND SUNDAY FREE TRAVEL.
VALID ONLY DURING WEEK OF ISSUE.

FOR OLD AGE PENSIONERS — LANCASHIRE COUNTY CONCESSIONARY FARES WILL BE VALID INTO SKIPTON.

Pennine Service
218

Gargrave · Barnoldswick · Earby · Gargrave, Johnson & Johnson Circular

Monday to Friday

Code	◆
Gargrave	0635
Thornton	0650
Coates Estate	0653
Barnoldswick	0655
Salterforth	0657
Kelbrook	0700
Earby	0703
Thornton	0707
Johnson & Johnson	0718
Gargrave	0720

Code	◆NF	◆F
Gargrave	1625	1225
Johnson & Johnson	1635	1235
Thornton	1649	1249
Earby	1652	1252
Kelbrook	1653	1253
Salterforth	1658	1258
Barnoldswick	1700	1300
Coates Estate	1702	1302
Thornton	1705	1305
Gargrave	1720	1320

Code: ◆ — Works service — liable to suspension if not so required. NF — Not Friday. F — Friday only.

PENNINE WAYFARER

£3.50 ADULT **£2.00 CHILD**

SETTING OFF FOR THE DAY — PAY ONCE AND TRAVEL ANYWHERE ON THE PENNINE BUS ROUTES. WHETHER YOU ARE GOING FROM SETTLE,SHOPPING INTO LANCASHIRE, OR TRAVELLING FROM LANCASHIRE TO THE YORKSHIRE DALES, RIDE TO MALHAM AND WALK OVER THE TOP TO SETTLE, AND CATCH THE BUS BACK FROM THIS BUSY MARKET TOWN. HOW ABOUT A TRIP TO INGLETON? FROM THIS PICTURESQUE VILLAGE FOLLOW THE FAMOUS WATERFALLS WALK — THIS FOUR AND A HALF MILE HIKE BY FOOTPATH THROUGH THE BEAUTIFUL INGLETON GLENS.

DO ALL THIS ON ONE DAILY WAYFARER TICKET.

Pennine Service
215

Skipton · Thornton · Earby · Colne · Nelson

Connections for Ribble services to Burnley and Manchester

Monday to Saturday

Code	◆	◆														◆
Skipton, Bus Station		0735	0835	0935	1035	1135	1235	1335	1435	1535	1635	1735	1905	2005	2105	2150
Thornton		0750	0850	0950	1050	1150	1250	1350	1450	1550	1650	1750	1920	2020	2120	2205
Barnoldswick, Con. Club	0644															
Earby, Bus Station	0653	0753	0853	0953	1053	1153	1253	1353	1453	1553	1653	1753	1923	2023	2123	2208
Kelbrook	0658	0758	0858	0958	1058	1158	1258	1358	1458	1558	1658	1758	1928	2028	2128	2213
Foulridge, Post Office	0703	0803	0903	1003	1103	1203	1303	1403	1503	1603	1703	1803	1933	2033	2133	2218
Colne, Bus Station	0707	0807	0907	1007	1107	1207	1307	1407	1507	1607	1707	1807	1937	2037	2137	2222
Nelson, Bus Station	0720	0820	0920	1020	1120	1220	1320	1420	1520	1620	1720	1820	1950	2050	2150	2235

Sunday

Code	*					
Skipton, Bus Station		1135	1335	1535	1735	2105
Thornton		1150	1350	1550	1750	2120
Barnoldswick, Con. Club	0944					
Earby, Bus Station	0953	1153	1353	1553	1753	2123
Kelbrook	0958	1158	1358	1558	1758	2128
Foulridge, Post Office	1003	1203	1403	1603	1803	2133
Colne, Bus Station	1007	1207	1407	1607	1807	2137
Nelson, Bus Station	1020	1220	1420	1620	1820	2150

* — Operates from the Fosters Arms 0939

Pennine Service
215

Nelson · Colne · Earby · Thornton · Skipton

Monday to Saturday

Code	*	*															◆	□◆
Nelson, Bus Station			0730	0830	0930	1030	1130	1230	1330	1430	1530	1630	1730	1830	2000	2100	2200	2240
Colne, Bus Station			0743	0843	0943	1043	1143	1243	1343	1443	1543	1643	1743	1843	2013	2113	2213	2253
Foulridge, Post Office			0748	0848	0948	1048	1148	1248	1348	1448	1548	1648	1748	1848	2018	2118	2218	2258
Kelbrook			0753	0853	0953	1053	1153	1253	1353	1453	1553	1653	1753	1853	2023	2123	2223	2303
Barnoldswick, Con. Club	0640	0703																2316
Earby, Bus Station	0649	0712	0757	0857	0957	1057	1157	1257	1357	1457	1557	1657	1757	1857	2027	2127	2227	2307
Thornton	0652	0715	0800	0900	1000	1100	1200	1300	1400	1500	1600	1700	1800	1900	2030	2130	2230	
Skipton, Bus Station	0707	0730	0815	0915	1015	1115	1215	1315	1415	1515	1615	1715	1815	1915	2045	2145	2245	

Sunday

Nelson, Bus Station	1030	1230	1430	1630	1830	2200
Colne, Bus Station	1043	1243	1443	1643	1843	2213
Foulridge, Post Office	1048	1248	1448	1648	1848	2218
Kelbrook	1053	1253	1453	1653	1853	2223
Barnoldswick, Con. Club						
Earby, Bus Station	1057	1257	1457	1657	1857	2227
Thornton	1100	1300	1500	1700	1900	2230
Skipton, Bus Station	1115	1315	1515	1715	1915	2245

Code: ◆ — Works service — liable to suspension if not so required.
* — Operates from the Fosters Arms, Barnoldswick at 0635 and 0658.
□ — Operates via Earby at 2307.
CHRISTMAS DAY, BOXING DAY AND NEW YEARS DAY — NO SERVICE.

Pennine Service
217

Skipton · Embsay · Eastby/Skipton · Carleton/Skipton · Horse Close Circular

Monday to Saturday

Code	◆	◆	◆	◆	◆	◆□		◆□									†	†					
Skipton, Bus Station		0640	0715			0810			0935		1020	1120	1220		1320	1420	1520	1540	1615			1735	
Embsay, Elm Tree		0647	0722			0817			0942		1028	1128	1228		1328	1428	1528		1623			1743	
Eastby, Masons Arms						0825			0950				1235						1630			1751	
Embsay, Elm Tree						0833			0958				1243						1637			1759	
Skipton, Regal					0752					0936	1036	1136		1236	1336	1436	1540						
Aireville, School						0842												1545					
Skipton, Bus Station		0656	0729	0735		0845			1005				1252						1645	1620	1735	1801	
Carleton, Centre		0705			0800		0831			0945	1045	1145		1245	1345	1445	1550			1630	1745		
Skipton, Bus Station	0635	0714			0810		0840	0825		0955	1055	1155		1255	1355	1455	1600	1555	1655	1640	1755		1740
Newmarket Street	0637			0736				0827		0957	1057	1157		1257	1357	1457		1557	1657				1742
Hurrs Road/Moorview Way	0639			0738				0829		0959	1059	1159		1259	1359	1459		1559	1659				1744
Shortbank Road/Hillside Crescent	0642			0741				0832		1002	1102	1202		1302	1402	1502		1602	1702				1747
Whinnygill	0644			0743				0834		1004	1104	1204		1304	1404	1504		1604	1704				1749
Horse Close Pub	0646			0745				0836		1006	1106	1206		1306	1406	1506		1606	1706				1751
Cawder Green	0648			0747				0838		1008	1108	1208		1308	1408	1508		1608	1708				1753
Skipton, Bus Station	0652			0752				0841		1012	1112	1212		1312	1412	1512		1612	1712				1757

Monday to Saturday continued

Code					⊕◆
Skipton, Bus Station	1820			2120	2215
Embsay, Elm Tree	1828			2127	2222
Eastby, Masons Arms					
Embsay, Elm Tree					
Skipton, Regal	1836			2136	2229
Aireville, School					
Skipton, Bus Station		2042			2235
Carleton, Centre	1845	2051		2145	2244
Skipton, Bus Station	1855	2100	2105	2155	
Newmarket Street	1857		2107		
Hurrs Road/Moorview Way	1859		2109		
Shortbank Road/Hillside Crescent	1902		2112		
Whinnygill	1904		2114		
Horse Close Pub	1906		2116		
Cawder Green	1908		2118		
Skipton, Bus Station	1912		2120		

Sunday

Skipton, Bus Station	1120		1420	1520	1720
Embsay, Elm Tree	1128		1428	1528	1728
Eastby, Masons Arms					
Embsay, Elm Tree					
Skipton, Regal	1136		1436	1536	1736
Aireville, School					
Skipton, Bus Station					
Carleton, Centre	1145		1445	1545	1745
Skipton, Bus Station	1155	1355		1555	1755
Newmarket Street	1157	1357		1557	1757
Hurrs Road/Moorview Way	1159	1359		1559	1759
Shortbank Road/Hillside Crescent	1202	1402		1602	1802
Whinnygill	1204	1404		1604	1804
Horse Close Pub	1206	1406		1606	1806
Cawder Green	1208	1408		1608	1808
Skipton, Bus Station	1212	1412		1612	1812

Code: ◆— Works service — liable to suspension if not so required. † — Operates via Wood Yard. □ — Continues to Aireville School. ⊕— Operates via Carleton and Earby to Barnoldswick.
CHRISTMAS DAY, BOXING DAY AND NEW YEARS DAY — NO SERVICE.

Extensive flooding occured in Skipton inJune 1979 when a cloud burst on Eastby Moor resulted in flooding in the Newmarket Street, Swadford Street and Keighley Road areas. This was directly caused by the mass of water passing down the Wilderness Beck in which flood this Pennine bus became trapped. Tony Edwards

YGE 635 was photographed at the Barnoldswick garage and was a 1978 Leopard purchased in 1986. Note the lack of ownership insignia. Tony Edwards

The following routes are currently(1999)worked by Pennine Motor Services:-

210 Skipton-Malham via Gargrave, Airton and Kirby Malham.- A weekdays only service
211 Skipton - Barnoldswick via Carleton and Thornton-in-Craven.
212 Skipton-Carleton.
214 Skipton-Embsay via Shires Lane.
215 Skipton-Burnley via Colne and Nelson.
216 Skipton - Horse Close circular.
218 Gargrave - Barnoldswick via Thornton-in-Craven and Earby.
580 Skipton-Giggleswick via Gargrave, Hellifield and Settle. - This service originally ran to Ingleton but now terminates at Giggleswick.

The Company also operates services to Johnson & Johnson's works in Gargrave from Skipton, Settle, Earby and Barnoldswick. Such was the patronage that seperate routes were operated from Barnoldswick and Earby with buses duplicated. Now these routes are combined and only one bus is needed. The Johnson & Johnson services were killed by the Government. In excess of 1000 people were employed at Johnson & Johnson's Gargrave factory and the Company subsidised the workers fares making bus travel attractive. Unfortunately the Government considered this subsidy to be a perk and accordingly taxed it and made it subject to National Insurance. The result - Pennine lost 200 passengers journeys each day and people travelled to work by car.

Recent competition has appeared on the Skipton - Malham route in the shape of a Postbus whose charges were less than Pennine fares and with losses guaranteed. Despite the fact that Pennine were running four journeys to Malham on Wednesdays and three on other days some bright spark went into the Post Office at York saying that there was no bus service to Malham. Accordingly the Post Office were paid to start up by the Countryside Commission and the Dales National Park. The result was the abandonment by Pennine of lunch-time turns and later by the withdrawal of all Saturday and Sunday buses, leaving only the school bus.

In 1993 Norman Simpson introduced a ramblers service from Burnley on summer Sundays to places like Bolton Abbey, Malham, Settle and Grassington. These were operated without subsidy at a special fare valid for use on these special routes Lancashire County Council arranged publicity circulating rambling clubs and similar but at the end of the 1996 summer season these services were abandoned - the best loading Pennine had had in 3 years was 7 passengers!

1991 marked a return to purchasing new rolling stock when two Leyland *Swift* buses with Reeves/Burgess 39-seat bodies were added to the fleet. Unfortunately these were to prove unsatisfactory and they were soon disposed of.

H313 WUA was the first of a pair of Leyland Swift buses purchased in 1991 but these were to prove unsatisfactory. The livery carried was all-over orange and this photograph was taken in Skipton Bus Station in June 1991. P.Lason

NEW PURCHASES 1991

Registration No.	Make	Chassis No.	Type	New	In to service.	Out of service.	Disposal
H313 WUA	Leyland Swift	LBM 0334	Reeves Burgess▲	4/91	4/91*	1/92	A
H314 WUA	Leyland Swift	LBM 0335	Reeves Burgess▲	4/91	4/91*	1/92	A

Disposal:

A. Sold to Stevenson's of Uttoxeter 1992. Sold because of inadequate brakes, poor quality work and inadequate after-sales service.

▲ Type DP39F   * Purchased New

A pair of Leyland Swift 39 seat buses were purchased new in 1991 but were sold in the following year because of a general dis-satisfaction - poor quality work, poor brakes and poor after sales service. The second of the pair - H314 WUA was photographed at Gargrave and differed from the first in that it was painted in the full Pennine bus livery of orange, black and gray.
Tony Edwards

A broadside view of H314 WUA in Skipton Bus Station. P & M Bewes collection

A rear view of Leyland Swift H314 WUA taken at Gargrave. Tony Edwards

Skipton bus station with a pair of Pennine Leyland/Plaxton vehicles and a Keighley & District National in the centre. YGE 635S(on the right)came to Pennine in 1986. JWU 798N on the left was new to Pennine in 1975.
P.Lason

With the 1990s came Irish registration plates. JIL 2426 had been BTL 485X and was photographed in Gargrave Road, Skipton in 1986.
P.Lason

Following this disappointment Pennine purchased a number of second-hand Leyland National buses and removed the roof-pods, intending to refurbish some and use others for spares. Four were fitted with Volvo TDH 100 engines and new back axles, all other work being undertaken by a Leeds firm and by Pennine at Gargrave. At the close of 1999 there are 13 Leyland National's in service numbered LN1 - LN12 and LN14 (the number 13 has not been used). All these plus the two surviving Leyland/Plaxton vehicles now carry Irish plates.

During the 1990s the fleet was given Irish registration plates and received, for the first time fleet numbers. Irish plates were carried by all the revenue earning fleet and all but the coach(BTL 485X)received fleet numbers. Several of the then surviving Leyland/Plaxton vehicles received Irish registration plates, but were withdrawn before fleet numbers were applied.

1. Leyland/Plaxtons known to have carried Irish plates:

Original Registration	Ulster Registration	Re-registration	Notes
UWR 712R	JIL 7417	None	On withdrawal plate used on LN8.
AUA 965S	JIL 7416	None	On withdrawal plate used on LN10.
OCK 452T	JIL 4653	HWR 449T	Converted to tow-truck. Plate used later on LN9.
OUF 50W	JIL 2427	None	Still owned by Pennine late 1999.
BTL 485X	JIL 2426	None	Still owned by Pennine late 1999.

2. Leyland/Plaxton known to have carried Irish plates and given fleet numbers:

Fleet No.			
12	NWT 839V	JIL 4698.	On withdrawal, plate used on LN11.
14	NPA 220W	JIL 2428	On withdrawal, plate used on LN12.

3. Leyland Nationals:

Fleet No.	Registration No.	Previous Registration No.	Make	Type
LN1	JIL 2794	SPC 282R	Leyland National	B44F*
LN2	RIB 5081	YPF 767R	Leyland National	B44F*
LN3	JIL 7422	SPC 276R	Leyland National	B44F*
LN4	JIL 2793	OJD 279R	Leyland National	B44F
LN5	JIL 2795	XDL 800L	Leyland National	B44F*
LN6	JIL 8353	PWY 583W	Leyland National	B44F
LN7	JIL 6502	OLS 807T	Leyland National	B44F
LN8	JIL 7417	OLS 809T	Leyland National	B44F
LN9	JIL4653	HPF 311N	Leyland National	B44F
LN10	JIL 7416	JNA 589N	Leyland National	B44F
LN11	JIL 4698	JCK 847W	Leyland National	B44F
LN12	JIL 2428	YPL 423T	Leyland National	B44F
LN13	Not used.			
LN14	JTU 599T	JTU 599T	Leyland National	B44F

LN1	New to London Country, bought from Northumbria.
LN2	New to London Country, bought from R& I Buses. RIB 5081 carried when purchased.
LN3	New to London Country ,bought from Northumbria.
LN4	New to London Buses, bought from? Had two passenger doors.
LN5	New to Southern Vectis, purchased from ?
LN6	New to West Yorkshire Road Car Company, bought from Harrogate & District.
LN7	New to Alexander Midland Scottish, bought from Stagecoach, Ribble.
LN8	New to Alexander Midland Scottish, bought from Stagecoach, Ribble.
LN9	New to London Country, bought from Yorkshire Terrier.
LN10	New to Greater Manchester PTE, bought from Yorkshire Terrier.
LN11	New to Ribble Motor Services, bought from Sragecoach, Ribble.
LN12	New to London Country, bought from London Country.
LN14	New to Crossville, bought from Northern Bus/Main Line.

Notes:
* Volvo engine.

4. Service vehicles:

HWR 449T(formerly OCK 452T) Leyland Leopard
Ex - Fishwick.Converted to recovery vehicle at Gargrave.

5. Stored vehicles for preservation:

MTD 235	1951	Leyland Royal Tiger coach
OWY 179K	1972	Leyland Leopard/Plaxton bus(ex-Laycocks).

Re-registered with Irish plates, JIL 2428 was photographed in Skipton bus station. This had previously been NPA 220W. P.Lason

A rear view of JIL 4698 and RIB 5081. **H.Meyer**

Early tickets were issued on a Bell Punch system followed by a Willebrew system as once used by Ribble, using white for single fares and pink for returns. On these the value was clipped out of a multi-value ticket. Later came the modern Setright tickets and then Almex manual. Pennine has currently invested in new Almex A90 ticket machines to replace all the older ones of the same make. In the Setright ticket period Pennine conductors paid in at Ribble offices but still kept their independence.

Both Leyland and Ford lorries have been used as breakdown/tow-trucks. A Ford Thames crane truck on trade-plates was replaced in 1985 by a Leyland Mercury flat truck with a crane, also on trade-plates. The current tow-truck is an ex-Fishwick Leyland/Plaxton coach registered OCK 452T and when converted was re-registered HWR 449T. This was re-built at Gargrave by cutting away the rear of the coach body and fitting the lifting gear from its predecessor.

The Simpson family have always been dedicated to providing the local community to the best of their ability, and at no expense to the rate payers, with rural bus services without any subsidy from either the North Yorkshire or the Lancashire County Councils. This was made possible because Pennine have various property holdings and have used the rents to subsidise the public with no help from Government, County or District until this year(1999)when Government made a payment to North Yorkshire in the form of a rural bus Grant for additional journeys, Pennine qualifying on the Malham route where the Post Bus does not run on either Saturdays or Sundays. Also on the Carleton and Barnoldswick routes. As readers of this book will realise all this has not always been easy but Norman Simpson is truly proud of his Company and of his loyal employee's numbering some two dozen. Something in the order of half-a-million miles are covered annually by Pennine buses, with only odd journeys missed.

Christmas Eve in the year 2000 will be the 75th Anniversary of Pennine Motor Services and the intention is that the Company will continue as a private concern - we hope it will still be under the direction of Norman Simpson and his son's, who, since 1994 have been Partners. As to future vehicles - when the current Leyland National programme is finished, Norman hopes to buy 30-seat Dennis *Dart's*. The 75th Anniversary

Pennines Leyland Leopard Plaxton-bodied coach had been re-registered JIL 2426 when photographed outside the Girls High School in Skipton.
H.Meyer

Old and newer in Skipton bus station. Leyland/Plaxton, Fleet No.12: JIL 4698 and Leyland National RIB 5081 - Fleet No.LN2. H.Meyer

might even witness the re-birth of the underfloor-engined Leyland *Royal Tiger* coach MTD 235 restored to her former magnificence. How nice it would be if the other stored vehicle Leyland *Leopard/* Plaxton UWY 179K could be restored into Ezra Laycock colours.

After the disappointments of the new Leyland Swifts Pennine decided to purchase used 44 seat Leyland Nationals and LN1 - JIL 2794 was the first. It was photographed in Skipton bus station in July 1994. P.Lason

LN2 already had Irish plates when it was purchased and these were retained. Photographed in Skipton bus station whilst waiting to work the town circular. Notice the blind to the right of the destination 'Pay on Entry, Exact Fare Please'! P.Lason

LN2 - RIB 5081 in a later photograph in Skipton bus station. Note that 'Pennine' has now been applied to the bus front.
H.Meyer

In early August 1999 two Pennine Leyland National's had orange painted front ends with parts picked out in more black than usual. LN11 was the first to be so treated and LN6 was the second. Both are different and this view shows the attractive appearance next to a standard front end paint job as applied to LN2. H.Meyer

LN6 - JIL 8353 had previously worked for the West Yorkshire Road Car Company and was recorded in Pennine ownership coming down the Bailey at the top of Skipton High Street. H.Meyer

LN9 - JIL 4653 in Skipton bus station about to work the Burnley route. P.Lason

LN4 - JIL 2793 pokes its nose out of the Skipton garage behind the Town Hall. P.Lason

LN4 on the Embsay - Skipton run passing beneath the branch railway to Swinden at the foot of Cross Bank.

H.Meyer

When LN6 received the new front end treatment a new style of ownership was applied to its rear. Gone was the Pennine scroll, replaced by 'Pennine Motor Services' in small black lettering placed centrally. The scroll insignia was however retained on the bus sides. H.Meyer

LN7 was put into service with its original registration OLS 807T and was seen in Skipton High Street in early August 1995. P.Lason

This is how LN6 looked until a 1999 repaint(illustrated next). P.Lason

When repainted in 1999 LN6 received the artistic touch at the front end with certain features picked out in black.

H.Meyer

JIL 4698 passing the Swan Inn at Carleton having diverted from the main road onto Heslaker Lane, then to Carleton, and forward to Skipton with this run from Barnoldswick.
H.Meyer

JIL 4698. This Irish plate was previously on a Leyland/Plaxton but as these were withdrawn the plates were re-used. This front end view at Skipton Bus Station shows the additional black decoration around the radiator and lights. H.Meyer

Later LN7 was re-registered JIL 6502 and was seen on Carleton New Road heading for Barnoldswick via Carleton. This vehicle was ex-Ribble.

H.Meyer

JIL 4698 - LN11 was photographed in rural setting en-route to Barnoldswick.

H.Meyer

Four Pennine Nationals in Skipton bus station. Left to right: LN5, LN2, LN11 and LN10 on the right. H.Meyer

This Leyland Mercury NDO 263M was a flat truck with a crane, introduced by Pennine in 1985 and used as a breakdown/tow truck.Pennine ownership was in black letters on the cab doors. Photographed at Gargrave. Tony Edwards

The current service vehicle is this Leyland Leopard obtained from Fishwick, Preston, and converted to a recovery vehicle at Gargrave. It is now HWR 449T and is seen about to recover a broken down Leyland National from Skipton bus station.

H.Meyer

About to start out for Gargrave with the broken down National. The towing vehicle carries Pennine orange and grey livery with a yellow front and black stripes. H.Meyer

LN2 suffering the indignity of being towed back to Gargrave where repairs will be effected. Just another days work for HWR 449T. H.Meyer

INTO THE 21st CENTURY

The following changes took place in the period September - December 1999.

In late September Pennine purchased three additional Leyland National 44-seat buses from Arriva(their No's 201/5/10). These are Volvo engined:

Registration No.	Pennine Fleet No.	Chassis No.
BYW 367V	LN16	06382
BYW 412V	LN17	06506
BYW 437V	LN15	06572

With the necessary work completed LN15 and LN16 entered service towards the end of October 1999 at which time LN7 was withdrawn with a suspect chassis, but is retained for spares and the fleet number left blank. LN17 entered service in 2000.

Another 44-seat National was purchased from Arriva (their No.206)in late 1999 and is again Volvo-engined.

BYW 413V	LN18	06507

So at 1 January 2000 Pennine had 16 Leyland Nationals and two Leyland Plaxtons. On the non-revenue earning side, the Company still have two vehicles ear-marked for possible preservation and of course the breakdown/tow truck converted from a Plaxton bodied bus.

In the year 2000 two further Volvo engined 44-seat Leyland National buses were purchased from Arriva:-

BYW 432V	LN19	06561
BYW 430V	LN20	06555

LN19 is expected to be on the road at the end of April 2001 followed by LN20 later in the Summer

A third vehicle was purchased in 2000 - this was a Leyland National engined 44-seater fitted out by previous owners as a disabled bus, but never used. It will be re-fitted by Pennine as a conventional service bus - Purchased from Derbyshire County Council AXI 7705 Chassis No.06469.

Only one bus was deleted in 2000 - this was LN9 registered JIL 4653. This plate was then transferred to LN16 which lost its BWY 367V identity and is now JIL 4653.

On the management side Norman Simpson's two sons John D. and Maurice B., joined the firm in 1990 as sleeping partners. In 2000 John D.Simpson BSc.ACMA remains a partner. Maurice B.Simpson BSc became a working partner at Gargrave alongside his father Norman.

Now with a grandson, perhaps a 4th generation of Simpsons will eventually keep the orange, black and grey buses running through the towns and Dales around Gargrave along with the routes in East Lancashire. With any sort of luck and good will Pennine will hopefully celebrate its centenary in the year 2025.

LOST! Unfortunately one volume of photographs belonging to Pennine has been lost. This contained early photographs, many in a small format. This album was inadvertently sent to a charity sale in Skipton along with other goods. Pennine Motors have advertised for the return of these pictures to no avail. I you know where they are please contact Mr N.Simpson, who will be extremely pleased to have them back. A reward is offered.

Two of the three latest arriv photographed at Gargrave in October 1999. H.Meyer(b